Community Councils and Community Control
The Workings of Democratic Mythology

Community Councils and Community Control

The Workings of Democratic Mythology

HAROLD H. WEISSMAN

University of Pittsburgh Press

ISBN 0-8229-3199-0
Library of Congress Catalog Card Number 75-101192
Copyright © 1970, University of Pittsburgh Press
All Rights Reserved
Manufactured in the United States of America

TO

ISABELLE LEVIN WEISSMAN

1904–1951

A GOOD CITIZEN

Contents

Tables

ABOUT THE AUTHOR

Harold H. Weissman is assistant executive director of Mobilization for Youth, Inc., in New York City. He is editor of the New Social Work series, a four-volume analytical history of this pioneer antipoverty agency, and author of articles in *Social Work Practice* and *Social Work*.

Acknowledgments

I AM especially indebted to several people for their help with this project. For his field assignment during his second year at the Columbia University School of Social Work, Dr. Irwin Epstein served as a research assistant in this project. No one could have been more helpful. His intelligence, dedication, and good wit made this period of the study the most rewarding intellectually and personally. I am also indebted to him for criticisms of the text.

Dr. Richard Cloward, former Director of Research of Mobilization for Youth, which financially supported this project, provided guidance in developing the conception on which the study is based. His suggestions and criticisms were extremely useful.

The major portion of this study was my doctoral dissertation. Dr. Simon Slavin served as my dissertation adviser. For his overall support I am appreciative.

Special recognition must be given to the staff worker of the council under study, whose pseudonym in the text is Martin Hill. He gave unsparingly of his time and energy to see that the study was carried out successfully. The text gives only passing notice to his integrity, high sense of purpose, and professional commitment. These qualities deserve more mention. In any case study only a small and select part of what transpired can be reported. Any criticisms made of Hill's performance must be viewed in the light of this perspective.

Jean Behrens and Betty Gillespie carried out some of the interviews of council participants. Their perseverance will be remembered and appreciated. I am also indebted to Paulman and Unhan, pseudonyms for the staff workers who followed Hill, for assistance in the latter stages of the study. Lenora Segal read final drafts of the text and made valuable suggestions. The clarity of thought in the volume was immeasurably aided by the editorial assistance of Louise Craft.

Last, and most importantly, I want to express my thanks to those citizens of Du Pont who gave so much time and effort to the Council and to me in carrying out the research. Though pseudonyms are used, they will know who they are in the text, which I hope conveys some measure of my admiration for their work.

Introduction

WHEN ALEXIS de Tocqueville first visited America in the early part of the nineteenth century, he was particularly impressed with the number of voluntary associations—civic, fraternal, and social. For him these associations were the backbone of American democracy, for in them citizens both learned the rules and procedures of democratic government and exerted an influence on that government.

De Tocqueville's visits occurred before social reformers had focused their attention on the urban slum environment. When this concern took hold at the beginning of the twentieth century, it was only natural, given the American tradition of voluntary associations, that one would be utilized to attempt to change existing conditions. These associations, social settlements, developed a variety of programs aimed at improving the slum environment.

One program, the most characteristically American, was the attempt to involve residents themselves in efforts to improve their lot. Though a number of different types of ad hoc associations were developed to deal with specific problems such as housing conditions or sanitation, just as often organizations were formed that dealt with the range of local problems. These organizations had a variety of names, such as block organizations, neighborhood councils, and community associations. They all shared somewhat the same structure and procedures; their memberships were open to residents or to representatives of local organizations or to some combination of both; their meetings and business were conducted according to democratic procedures. They also all shared the same goal, which was some form of community improvement and control over housing conditions, schools, recreational facilities, etc. This goal was to be achieved through processes at various times called citizen participation, community involvement, and community control, all of which stood in varying degrees for the right of citizens to make decisions about community affairs.

The results achieved by these organizations have not in general been impressive. As one observer noted, "America is a graveyard for community councils under whatever name or sponsorship they may have appeared. More often than not community councils have followed a rather well-established cycle from birth to a splurge of enthusiasm and activity, to sudden death or at best gradual disintegration."[1]

The major intent of this study is to develop a model for understanding how neighborhood councils and other voluntary civic organizations operate and to suggest how they might be more effective in achieving their ends. The focus of this study, the Du Pont Neighborhood Council, was committed to various forms of *community control* from its inception in the middle 1950s. As the history of this council is related, the change in the degree of community control advocated—from local citizens suggesting and urging to ordering and administering—will be obvious. Nevertheless, the study is not directed primarily at determining whether specific types of control were either good or bad in Du Pont but rather to demonstrate how a voluntary citizens' organization can be utilized to exercise this control. However, implicit in the model developed is a means of judging some of the effects of such attempts on communities as well as their possibility of success.

History of Neighborhood Councils

Several currents in social work itself led to the development of neighborhood councils. The earliest was characterized by the thinking of such people as Jane Addams, who believed that the physical and social environment must be changed if people are to improve their own lives. Others in the settlement-house movement believed that people must be taught to take responsibility for themselves, their lives, and their government. Neighborhood councils were the natural outgrowth of both the social-reform and education orientations. Through the council each citizen was to be given the opportunity and means of participating in efforts to change his physical and social environment.

World War I gave great impetus to cooperative civic ventures in cities and towns throughout the country. War bond drives and the like were carried on by community and neighborhood organizations and were in the main successful. From 1917 to 1919 the Cincinnati Social Unit Experiment, a total effort to organize a neighborhood block by block as well as by occupation, was attempted.[2] The experiment floundered as a result of lack of financial support and opposition from the existing citywide power structure. Not only was the enthusiasm engendered among social workers by the experiment considerably dampened, but hope began to fade that an adequate social mechanism had really been devised to meet the problems of working-class neighborhoods. Nevertheless, the 1920s saw the rise of an adult-education movement, which placed strong emphasis on citizens' taking responsibility for their government.

Since World War II led to a tremendous growth of citizens' organizations for neighborhood civilian-defense campaigns, scrap collections, and war bond drives, more people than ever before gained experience in community action. As a result, after the war the idea of establishing a council in each neighborhood gained acceptance in cities. Although these councils were to be represented in a citywide council, no city ever completely achieved this pyramid type of council organization.

However, some cities, such as Kansas City, went so far as to pay welfare department staff to act as advisers for the neighborhood councils that the department organized. Many councils in many cities were begun and died. Even so, some of the short-lived ones performed important services, such as keeping a changing neighborhood from erupting into racial violence and preventing gang warfare.[3] A few councils survived and remained effective forces in their neighborhoods.

In the early 1960s there were two divergent opinions in the field of community organization: one fervently contended that neighborhood councils could help realize the great ideals of social democracy if their membership were broadened to include representatives of all groups in a neighborhood, rather than simply representatives from social agencies. The other held that neighborhood councils were an impractical, idealistic solution to the problems faced by the poor and uneducated in our urban slums.[4] This disagreement within the profession over the utility of neighborhood councils was epitomized in the position of two social agencies located in the area in which this study takes place: HEED (Higher East End Development), championing neighborhood councils, and OPUS (Organization for the Planning of Urban Services), taking the contrary view. The differences between these two agencies paralleled to some degree the political conflict between the classical municipal reformers and "good government" group on the one hand and the "party politics" group on the other hand.

The reform ideal in politics has generally emphasized three planks: eliminating corruption, increasing efficiency, and making local government more democratic.[5] These ideals are deeply enmeshed in the ideology of neighborhood councils. Rationality, planning, and mutual understanding of all groups was the concern of HEED. OPUS on the other hand sought to organize people in its area in ways that would maximize their power and enhance their position in striking political bargains with citywide centers of decision making. This agency was, then, more interested in organizing power such as might be developed in ethnic groups, the unaffiliated, the poor, than in having all segments of the population represented in one organization.

Both groups could claim support for their position on neighborhood councils from the few existing studies since the results reported in the studies were often ambiguous. A study of four councils in St. Louis showed that the only one that exerted significant influence on its neighborhood was the council that received no service from professional staff.[6] Sower and his associates found that after the death of a health council, what remained was a pattern of interpersonal relationships that often served as an informal means of community problem-solving that could be quickly reactivated for formal purposes when required.[7]

Selection of the Study Area

To understand better the utility of neighborhood councils as mechanisms for solving urban problems, one of HEED's councils, Du Pont, was selected for study. The primary reason for this selection was that Du Pont corresponded to the ideal type of neighborhood council. It was staffed by a professionally trained social worker. Membership was open to citizens and organizations in the area. There was a formal structure of committees and officers. The membership made the decisions and carried out the programs of the council by democratic procedure and vote. The council was dedicated to a program that stressed equal opportunities and responsibility in community affairs for neighborhood residents.

In addition, the Du Pont Neighborhood Council had already been in existence for nearly seven years and could boast of an impressive number of community accomplishments. It also had an extensive set of records of its activities. The council was affiliated with the area-wide organization HEED, one of the leading proponents of neighborhood councils as a means of solving urban problems. Under the terms of a grant that furnished the bulk of its budget, HEED was under obligation to engage in research.[8]

The relationship of a council to its environment is obviously important. From this point of view, the Du Pont neighborhood presented a rich and intriguing source of data. Located in the heart of a large eastern metropolis, in eight square blocks it contained all the elements of a classic melting pot neighborhood. There were five distinct ethnic groups: Chinese, Italians, Puerto Ricans, Jews, and Negroes, with smaller numbers of Greeks, Irish, Basques, Armenians, and Slavs— twenty thousand people in all. There were tenements and street-corner societies, public and middle-income housing. Republicans and Democrats, regulars and reformers, made up its political life. There was a history of teen-age warfare and interracial tension. Buchanan Street was rumored to be one of the racket centers of the city, and Harold Street was a known haven for addicts. Yet when the white, Negro, and Chinese Little Leaguers held their annual, council-sponsored parade, the atmosphere was more like a small midwestern town than an inner-city slum.

The Exchange Model

Much of what has been written about neighborhood councils is a journalistic attempt to show the value of such councils.[9] In seeking to demonstrate this value, the failures of councils have seldom been explored. In addition, almost all studies of neighborhood councils or like structures have been conducted ex post facto. This approach is limited, for it restricts research to those problems and cases for which adequate records or data exist. If an important population segment is absent, or a crucial variable not recorded, or events simply forgotten, the gap cannot be filled when the study is undertaken. Most of the existing studies also lack systematic rigor and are unrelated to existing theoretical formulations about organizational functioning. Sower's study of a community health council was an exception, however, for he discarded the retrospective approach and attempted to describe what had occurred in conceptual terms. (See note 7.)

The present study was motived by the desire to describe council functions in analytic terms. First, because it was to be a study of a single case, generalizations derived would have to be tested in other councils. To do this, concepts were needed. Secondly, the researchers were strongly committed to describing a council so as to provide future staff workers with guidelines for action. The goal was operable variables that would add most to practice knowledge.[10]

To a certain extent, any case study is open to the charge that the researchers observed and recorded only that which fit into their pre-existing biases or theoretical orientations.[11] This study of Du Pont began without any one preconceived theory of council functioning. Observations and interviews were analyzed in terms of various conceptions. The purpose was not to test, revise, or develop new psychological or sociological theories, but to relate what happened in Du Pont to a set of existing concepts and to explore how these concepts might be applied to the problems of practice in neighborhood councils.

Ultimately an exchange model for understanding organizational interaction was selected. In this model voluntary organizations are viewed as *mechanisms in which individuals, organizations, and groups invest resources in the hope of securing a variety of rewards.* The chief utility of this view, one which depicts social behavior as a form of exchange, lies in the common denominator that it provides for understanding human interaction. It links individual and organization, person and group, council and neighborhood. Such an integrative concept is especially important for community workers, who must have some means of conceptualizing the dynamics of community and organizational life.

The first section of this study begins with a brief overview of the Du Pont neighborhood and its council to familiarize the reader with the context in which the exchanges occurred. An analysis of the exchange model is then presented, as well as a review of the traditional model of neighborhood councils. Following this section is a description of Du Pont's activities in the analytic terms of the model. The third section explores the contributions of the exchange model to practice knowledge in the field of community organization. The epilogue discusses changes in the council in the light of the newer meanings attached to the idea of community control.

NOTES

1. Gordon Blackwell, "A Theoretical Framework for Sociological Research in Community Organization," *Social Forces*, XXXIII (October 1954), 60.
2. Jesse Frederick Steiner, "The Cincinnati Social Unit Experiment," *Community Organization in Action*, eds. Ernest B. Harper and Arthur Dunham (New York: Association Press, 1959), pp. 117–26.
3. For a history of the development of the neighborhood council idea see Sidney Dillick, *Community Organization for Neighborhood Development* (New York: William Morrow and Company, 1953).
4. The usual criticisms are: (1) the poor do not join; (2) the council structure is inherently unsuited to engaging in conflict and, therefore, cannot help to alter those structural arrangements in society that militate against the poor; and (3) a council, because of its neighborhood location, can never have the power to influence city government or large bureaucracies.

5. See Edward C. Banfield and James Q. Wilson, *City Politics* (Cambridge: Harvard University Press and M.I.T. Press, 1963), pp. 138–50.
6. K. V. Sridharan, "Area Approach to Social Welfare Planning," (Ph.D. diss., Ohio State University, 1959), p. 66.
7. Christopher Sower et al., *Community Involvement* (Glencoe, Ill.: Free Press, 1957), pp. 288–90.
8. Another council, which was first being organized under the auspices of HEED, SECA, was also selected for study. But this organization, owing to a number of factors, did not really materialize as a council during the first year of the study. The intended comparative possibilities, in most cases, were not realized.
9. See for example Julia Abrahamson, *A Neighborhood Finds Itself* (New York: Harper and Bros., 1959); *Neighbors Unite for Better Communities: A Hand-Book on District Councils* (New York: United Community Funds and Councils of America, 1956); "Neighborhood Community Organization," *Community*, XXIII (May 1948), 185–86; *A Neighborhood Acts: An Experiment in Cooperative Neighborhood Rehabilitation* (New York: National Federation of Settlements and Neighborhood Centers, 1957).
10. For a discussion of the need for operable variables in social work, see Edwin J. Thomas, "Selecting Knowledge from Behavioral Science," *Building Social Work Knowledge* (New York: National Association of Social Workers, 1964), pp. 38–47.
11. In mitigation of this charge is the fact that the conceptions dealt with in this study were arrived at only after a long process of analysis of alternatives and only after the observations had been in process for a complete program year.

Part I

Neighborhood and Council

1

Du Pont and
Its Neighborhood

IN 1955–1956, when the Du Pont Neighborhood Council came into existence, its neighborhood was reacting violently to an influx of Negroes and Puerto Ricans. What had been an old Italian neighborhood, comfortable in its traditions and culture, accomodated to a small group of Jews living in its midst, was suddenly a multiracial neighborhood. Its difficulties were dramatized on its streets one summer night in the late 1950s.

For years, the Society of San Rocco, sponsored by one of the local churches, had held an annual street fair to raise money. On this summer night gang warfare erupted during the festival. The neighborhood was visibly shaken, and the festival was not held again until the summer of 1964. This intervening period may be regarded as the years of transition from the old, closed Italian neighborhood to one considerably more open to other ethnic groups.

Du Pont's mission in these intervening years was to open up the neighborhood, to make local institutions responsive to the needs not only of Italians and Jews, but also of Negroes, Puerto Ricans, and Chinese. To this end it staked out certain areas of activity—politics, health, education, recreation, housing—and then went about extending its influence in these spheres. The how and the why of Du Pont's successes and failures must begin with a description of the neighborhood and a brief history of the council's activities as a prelude to understanding how the council entered into exchanges to achieve its ends.

The Neighborhood

Located near City Hall, the Du Pont neighborhood is one of the oldest sections of the metropolis. First inhabited by Indians in early colonial times, then incorporated into a farm owned by one of our Founding Fathers, the area became a thriving trading center in the early nineteenth century. Its eastern boundary was lined with piers where boats put in with fish from Massachusetts, cocoa and coffee from the Indies, and sugar and cotton from the South. So many bars and second-rate hotels sprang up to cater to the needs of the transient sailors that the area soon became known as one of the most disreputable in the country.

Toward the end of the century, commerce in the area diminished. The streets became lined with tenements, peopled by immigrants. First came the Irish, then smaller numbers of Greeks; at the turn of the century came the Italians. By 1930 the neighborhood was predominantly Italian. Its eight square blocks were lined with Italian groceries, bakeries, social clubs, barber shops, and a host of other stores, along with pushcarts and sidewalk stands. Italian was heard more frequently than English.

In the mid 1930s the first of several physical changes in the area took place. A two-block square of tenements was demolished, and in its place was built a large government-subsidized private apartment development. This new housing brought for the first time a large group of Jews into the area. A more important change in relation to the development of the council occurred in 1949, when a public-housing project was begun. With the opening of its doors, considerable numbers of Puerto Ricans and Negroes took the place of the former Italian residents. In this same period large numbers of Chinese started to move into both the public-housing project and the tenements.

By September 1962, when this study began, the neighborhood contained approximately twenty thousand people, including roughly four thousand Italians, thirty-five hundred Puerto Ricans, two thousand Chinese, two thousand Negroes, and two thousand Jews, with a smattering of Greeks, Basques, Irish, English, and almost every other nationality conceivable. Within its eight-block square, there was a large public-housing development, a middle-income development, a middle-income cooperative, and several hundred tenements.

There were two public elementary schools, a junior high, and two parochial schools, all with parents' associations. The three fifths of the area's residents who were Roman Catholic were served by two large

Catholic churches, with another on the periphery. The four Protestant missions—one Baptist, one Methodist, one Presbyterian, and one Anglican—catered almost exclusively to Negroes and Puerto Ricans. There was a synagogue nearby, as well as a Chinese Presbyterian church and a storefront Pentecostal church. Jefferson House, the one remaining settlement house, served mainly Negro and Puerto Rican children.

The vast majority of families were working class and derived their income from sources outside the neighborhood. Although many of the small stores in the area were owned by local people (mainly Italians), there was no businessmen's association and no evidence of concern for community improvement on the part of local businessmen as a group.

Traditionally, the area has been Democratic by about four to one. In a recent contest for Democratic party leadership, the reformer was beaten by a more than three-to-one margin. The regular Democratic club, as well as the regular Republican club, was dominated by Italians and Jews, who in general had higher incomes and had been in the area longer. A majority of the people in the Du Pont neighborhood still looked to the clubhouse for help with problems of unemployment, housing, and the like.

As indicated earlier, five large ethnic subcommunities existed in Du Pont and their activities, aspirations, and interests dominated the neighborhood. A closer look at each of the five follows:[1]

The Italians

The Italian community has undergone drastic changes since the early 1930s and has been reduced from twenty thousand people to about four thousand. The first middle-income project replaced a large number of Italian homes, and the public-housing project displaced almost half the Italian community. Over the years numbers of Italians have worked for the city in sanitation, parks, etc. In addition, the city fish market was nearby, and a man could get a job there if he knew the right neighborhood politician.

In the main Du Pont Italians were suspicious of politics and regarded it as a dirty business. Nonetheless, if they were in economic or legal trouble, the "club" was still the place to go. New groups, like the council or reform political groups, were widely thought to be under Communist influence.

Religion was a vital factor. The two Roman Catholic churches maintained parochial schools with almost 100 percent enrollment from the Italian community. Both churches had active parent-teacher associations and Holy Name Societies and evoked considerable interest and devotion from their members.

The priests did not generally take part in community activities and seemed to represent only latent power in the community. However, older residents remembered a priest who had walked the streets and, with community sanction, delivered a beating to any child or teen-ager whose actions he disapproved. In the main, the Italian community felt that the church was good for children and adolescents; however, if the youngsters did not accept it, the church was not considered to be at fault. Social workers were suspect; and the settlement house had been deserted by the Italian community, which felt that this agency catered to Negroes and Puerto Ricans.

Social life among the Italians in the neighborhood was rich. In the summer the sidewalks were lined with chairs, the stoops were crowded, and there was much neighboring among families, who tended to see other groups in the neighborhood as outsiders.[2] A group of older teen-agers had in the past taken it upon themselves to protect the Italian community. When an Italian was bothered by a member of another ethnic group, these toughs retaliated against the group rather than the individuals concerned. Their behavior was not sanctioned by all, but there were those in the Italian community who felt that they kept the Negroes from running rampant over the neighborhood.

The Puerto Ricans

Puerto Ricans constituted the second largest ethnic group in the area and were concentrated in the public-housing project. By and large they liked the project and the neighborhood; both were viewed as an improvement over their life elsewhere. Most of the adults were born in Puerto Rico and did not speak English well.

One of their main problems was the getting and holding of a job, and the typical pattern was for both the men and the women to work. Sizable numbers were employed in the garment industry, where work was often seasonal.

School was the one area of community life outside the project with which Puerto Ricans were concerned. However, language presented a problem in discussions with teachers, as well as in their participation in the parents' associations. The average Puerto Rican was not awake politically. If he voted, he was probably a Democrat.

In the early 1960s a Spanish Adult Club was formed in the settle-ment house. Yet Puerto Rican leaders felt that the Spanish-speaking people needed a social outlet—a place where they could hold social functions and come together to talk—outside of the restrictions of church and settlement house. These leaders strongly desired to be part of the community, but felt that because the Puerto Rican group was not integrated within itself, it was not yet ready to participate in community affairs.

Some of the lack of integration of the Puerto Rican group within itself, as well as its lack of attachment to the community, might have been due to its lack of connection with its traditional church. Although the majority of Puerto Ricans were Roman Catholic, the local Catholic churches were not quick to respond to them. The Anglican, Methodist, and Presbyterian missions succeeded in recruiting substantial numbers of Puerto Ricans, many of whom also went to church outside the neighborhood. After considerable agitation the Irish Catholic church delivered one mass a week in Spanish, and during 1963 a Catholic church on the outskirts of the area began to work with Puerto Ricans, conducting services in Spanish and catering almost exclusively to the needs of this group. Of all the neighborhood groups, the Puerto Ricans seemed the most adrift.

The Puerto Ricans seemed shocked by the negative attitude of some of their neighbors toward them, and they were not completely happy about being associated with Negroes in the minds of the rest of the community. However, there seemed to be little overt tension among these two groups. Negro and Puerto Rican teen-agers mixed and in the past had been forced to stick together in battles with the Italians.

The Chinese

Du Pont contained about two thousand Chinese. Basically their orientation was toward a large Chinese district bordering on the Du Pont area. Ninety-five percent of the adults were born in China, and the majority did not speak English well. Most of the men worked in the countless Chinese restaurants ringing the area. Wives were often considerably younger than the husbands. The extended family was still important—family groups went on outings, visited family burial grounds, and adjudicated disputes. Outside of the extended family there seemed to be some, although not much, neighboring among the women.

Some women belonged to the Chinese New Life Movement, essentially a social organization based in the Chinese area. There were also several social clubs for older men, which served a free meal each day and where card playing was the major activity. In addition, the settlement house ran a golden-age program for elderly Chinese that attracted people from within and outside the area.

Religion did not seem to play a vital part in the lives of the Du Pont Chinese, although most of them were affiliated with one or another of the Christian churches located in the Chinese section bordering the area. They went to church for the other-than-religious services it offered, such as helping them to learn English, sending the children to camp, but the churches seemed to exert little influence on them.

The Chinese were not politically active in the area. In general, the adult group did not have a concept of citizenship that included participation in community affairs. In contrast, the children attended public school, played with the children of the other groups, and in most respects seemed to be a typical second-generation group. In 1964 a Chinese catcher was the top player in the Little League.

The real leadership of the Chinese community lay in the Chinese district bordering on Du Pont. For the Chinese adult Du Pont seemed to be only a convenient dormitory. Other groups in the area believed that the Chinese wished to be left alone and regarded them as hardworking people. The Chinese for their part had negative feelings toward the Negroes and Puerto Ricans, who they felt were responsible for some of the violence and petty thefts that had occurred in the neighborhood. These attitudes, as well as the language problem, kept association between the Chinese and other groups to a minimum.

The Negroes

Negroes began moving into the fringes of the Du Pont area toward the end of World War II. Their tenements were the most dilapidated in the area. A considerable percentage of the families were unstable, with few working husbands. By 1965 the majority of the two thousand Negroes lived in the public-housing development that replaced the tenements demolished in the late 1950s, and by and large, the housing project had a good reputation with them. For many Negroes their economic problem was inherent in the seasonal aspect of their work. Many were employed in the garment industry. Most of the unstable families were welfare recipients.

Politically, the neighborhood came alive for the Negroes in 1962. Prior to that time their vote had not been much in demand. However, in 1962 primary fights in both parties gave Negroes a chance for recognition.

Their formal integration into religious institutions came considerably easier. However, in the main the Negroes who moved to the neighborhood came with a tradition of emotionalized religion; the Protestant ministers who greeted them were schooled in the liberal, intellectual, humanitarian tradition. For some Negroes this transition was a shock. The churches were described as dead churches, and many returned to their old neighborhoods for church. Nevertheless, the majority sent their children to the local Protestant churches, which had extensive youth programs.

Some people felt bitterness at having no choice but to conform to the churches, but those active in neighborhood groups felt they had gained something from this experience: namely, the conviction that they had a religious responsibility for community affairs. On the other hand, large numbers of Negro adults had little connection with religion. A small percentage attended the local Catholic churches, and the Jehovah's Witness movement seemed to be growing.

Many Negroes in the area felt that they had no social outlet. The churches were not suitable for social functions, and people were fed up with just work. They were looking for things to do and would have been ready to join groups had opportunities been available. Several informants concurred that after many years of not feeling a part of anything, Negroes were beginning to feel that they belonged.

Those with middle-class orientations appeared to have a view of themselves as responsible for community affairs. Recognition of the need for education had taken hold among this group, and Negro women were active in the parents' associations.

The Jews

The influx of Jews came in the mid 1930s and early 1940s. In 1965 the population numbered about five hundred families and was centered in the older middle-income development. Since this housing project faced onto a large courtyard, there was a certain natural isolation from the rest of the community. Many of the original Jews who had moved in had a labor, socialist tradition. The rest included many city employees and owners of small businesses.

The Jews were active politically. Both the regular Democrats and Republicans had Jewish co-leaders, though most Jews were regular Democrats. For many years the parents' associations had Jewish leadership. Participation in community affairs was an accepted form of activity for Jews.

In a sense religion unified the Jews, but it did not seem to be a vital force in their lives. The area had never had a synagogue. In the mid 1960s one was built by city employees near the civic center, which adjoined Du Pont.

Most of the Jews fell into the older age group; there were few children. Since there were limited opportunities for their children to associate with other Jewish children, in the past many parents had moved elsewhere in the city. One informant felt that two hundred more families would leave within another year. The fact that Negroes and Puerto Ricans had moved into the area might also have been a contributing factor, although the Jews were more likely than the Italians to state that Negroes should be given their rights.

Socially the Jews were friendly with the Italians, although there was some latent strain between the two groups. Some Jews felt that one insurgent Italian Republican leader was anti-Semitic. In 1962 there was an incident of violence between the groups, which was quickly quieted by both Jewish and Italian politicians. In 1965 there were three Jewish women's groups in the area: one associated with the synagogue, two with Zionist orientations. There were no men's organizations, although the men collected money for the United Jewish Appeal once a year.

The Jews were tied into the neighborhood through politics and the schools and had taken positions of leadership in greater proportion than their numbers would indicate. They seemed to feel that the community affected their lives (that is, if prejudice were allowed to run rampant, they would be hurt). In addition, there was tangible evidence that Jews could affect the community through the leadership positions they held. The rapid cooling off of the one violent action between Jews and Italians gave credence to this point of view.

The remaining groups in the neighborhood were hardly noticeable. There were still numbers of Irish affiliated with the Irish Catholic church, although Italians now dominated it. A remnant of a once large Basque community remained. The old Basque men maintained a card-playing club. All that remained of the Greeks were a couple of second-hand stores and a ramshackle coffeehouse where they gathered.

History of the Du Pont Council

The Du Pont Council came into existence in this neighborhood during the autumn and winter of 1955–1956. At that time fighting gangs of Negro and white teen-agers ruled the streets, and vandalism was common. Suspicion, hostility, and prejudice ruled. Adults were frightened; and the police were overwhelmed with the magnitude of the problems, as these situations were also occurring in most of the areas adjacent to Du Pont.

The schools were overcrowded and deteriorating. The influx of Negro and Puerto Rican children was severely taxing the physical facilities of the schools. In addition, many of these children were neither adequately prepared nor sufficiently motivated for the kind of teaching offered by the public school. Longtime, middle-class residents became concerned that their children were having reading difficulties and that the quality of instruction was being dragged down. A group of these parents attempted with little success to get the city to institute remedial-reading classes. When they asked the director of Jefferson House for help, he suggested that other community leaders and staff workers be consulted. This action led to the formation of a remedial-reading committee.

A second crucial event occurred at about the same time, when the city proposed doing away with Johnson Oval, the only playing field in the area. The oval had been used primarily by Parish House, a Catholic settlement that has since been disbanded. The sister in charge contacted the director of Jefferson House, who once again suggested the formation of a broad-based community committee to deal with this problem, as well as with the overall problem of youth in the neighborhood.

The success of this recreation committee in blocking the city's plans for Johnson Oval and the unprecedented remedial-reading program inaugurated through the efforts of the remedial-reading committee led to the formation in March 1956 of the Du Pont Neighborhood Council. It stood for equal treatment for all and general improvement in neighborhood conditions and facilities. All community groups were invited to join, as were interested individuals. An executive and other functional committees, such as education and recreation, were formed.

In 1956 the neighborhood problem-solving organizations that might have competed with Du Pont were at a loss to deal with the many social problems they faced. The local political clubs were operating on an individual-by-individual problem-solving basis—that is, procuring food for a poor family, interceding with the police for a boy in trouble, finding a job for a laid-off worker. The Third Precinct Youth Council, which had been concerned with delinquency, had been disbanded. Other institutions—churches, schools, the police department, the housing authority—all had a history of concern for their own organization rather than for the community at large.

1956–1957

At the outset the Du Pont Council had considerable encouragement and support from local individuals and organizations. The director of Jefferson House served as the first president. Remedial-reading classes were held at the settlement house. Members of local parents' associa-

tions were recruited into the education committee, which succeeded
in securing after-school supervised recreation at one of the public
schools. Since delinquency was the major problem during the first year,
a rumbles committee, composed of citizens and agency personnel, was
formed to head off major conflicts between gangs. It coordinated the
efforts of all interested people in the area and is credited with averting
many near-disasters, although one boy was shot to death during this
time. The rumbles committee remained active during all the years of
gang conflict.

There was successful agitation for street lights in the darker sections
of the area. The housing committee helped citizens to face the problems of relocation caused by demolition for an area housing development. The health committee discussed fluoridation. Sports became an
active part of the council's program; and efforts by the sports committee to persuade the local Roman Catholic churches to participate
were successful, as was the resulting Little League program. With the
cooperation of the city's Youth Board, dances were held during the
summer. The staff worker, a Negro and a Catholic, was extremely well
liked in the community and was, without question, the central figure
in the council. Two unsuccessful ventures were a conference on teen
employment and a youth council.

1957–1958

In 1957 a local Italian druggist was elected president. The education
committee successfully pressed for a cafeteria in the junior high school
and protested the threatened closing of an elementary school. In addition, it successfully pushed for after-school recreation at a second elementary school. A committee was formed to deal with the growing
problem of narcotics. The housing committee successfully petitioned
for traffic lights on certain street corners and set up a housing clinic to
deal more comprehensively with housing and relocation problems. The
council became affiliated with HEED (Higher East End Development), the area-wide organization of neighborhood councils and institutions, but remained autonomous as far as decision-making.

1958–1959

The health committee surveyed the health needs of the community
and publicized a campaign for polio shots. Gaining in stature, the education committee discussed the issues of bonus pay for teachers and the
ratio of substitutes to regular teachers. It also began yearly appearances at the city council when it presented the needs of the local

schools. The community newspaper, formerly put out by members of the housing project and the middle-income development, was taken over by the council, and its circulation was expanded. A narcotics information center was established. The major event of the year was a Town Hall forum on gang warfare, attended by more than four hundred people. The regular Republican leader acted as moderator, and Democrats as well as Republicans showed up in force. Politicians began to attend other council functions. Membership in the council reached 100 and fluctuated from 75 to 125 in the years that followed.

1959–1960

A local Italian lawyer was elected president. The education committee sponsored a UNICEF carnival, which became a yearly event, and a career-day conference for teen-agers. As a fund-raising device the sports committee organized a parade. All the local politicians turned out, and the parade became a yearly event. The sports committee had previously inaugurated the giving of trophies and awards to almost all Little Leaguers. The local Democratic leader began giving a yearly donation of one hundred dollars, for which he was accorded the honor of making the awards at the end of the season.

Conferences were held with the police department about more protection, and the health committee organized a home-nursing course and attempted to set up a blood bank. A new staff worker interested the housing committee in developing an urban-renewal plan, which subsequently earned an award from a citywide professional planning group. The housing committee also helped to block the eviction of tenants from a site to be cleared for public housing until adequate relocation facilities could be worked out.

1960–1961

The education committee continued its agitation for new schools in the area. Not only was a program to train school volunteers instituted, but a workshop was held for parents on how to improve the reading skills of their children. In addition, the local school superintendent accepted the committee's suggestion to add Spanish books to the school libraries. The health committee expressed concern about the lack of school nurses and the poor treatment residents were receiving at the local hospital. Agitation was started for a new hospital in conjunction with HEED. There was considerable concern about teen-age drinking, and a Town Hall meeting on narcotics drew a small crowd. An extensive summer recreation program for teen-agers was organized.

TABLE 1

Du Pont Programs, 1962–1963

Education	Deviancy
Adult education	Filth and noise
Homework helpers	Police relations
Replacement of PS 4	Rumbles committee
Replacement of JH 13	
UNICEF carnival	Social
Brotherhood Week	Office opening
Board of estimate depositions	Going-away dinner
Visit to legislature	
	Health
Finances	Home nursing course
Trailer fund	School health exams
Canister campaign	Blood bank
	Health directory
Newspaper	Sex education
Five issues	Health questionnaire
	Drug legislation
Housing	Recreation
Civic center	Summer program
Garibaldi Park	Little League
Du Pont urban renewal	Sports parade
Harold Street Strip	
Ditch Street	Others
Boundary Street	Civil rights
Jones Softball Field	Consumer fraud

1961–1962

A young Jewish lawyer was elected president. The education committee petitioned the board of education for a Higher Horizon program, and a highly successful brotherhood celebration was held, with all public and parochial schools participating. It became a yearly event. However, a Town Hall meeting on fallout shelters was a complete failure, and Town Hall meetings were discontinued. Countless meetings were held with city officials about an urban-renewal plan for the neighborhood, which the city accepted in principle. A subcommittee was formed to help tenants on John Street to deal with housing problems, and the residents of the new middle-income cooperative were greeted by a welcoming-day celebration. Through the personal contact of a past president, a $1,400 grant was received from a philanthropic foundation.

During 1962–1963, when most of the major observations of this study were made, Du Pont engaged in many varied activities. See table 1.

Although Blackwell was no doubt accurate in noting that America has been a graveyard for neighborhood councils, when this study began, Du Pont was by no means ready for interment. It had remained alive for over six years and had as impressive a list of accomplishments for a council as the most ardent supporters of neighborhood councils could claim. The exchange model, to be described in the next chapter, will serve as the basis for the analysis of this success.

NOTES

1. Descriptive data on the ethnic groups were obtained by interviewing longtime residents, most of whom were not active members of Du Pont, but whom key informants felt to be knowledgeable about their group. These descriptions reflect conditions in 1965.
2. For a description of relations among groups in a multi-ethnic neighborhood in Chicago, see Gerald Suttles, *The Social Order of the Slum* (Chicago: University of Chicago Press, 1968).

2

An Analytical Model
of a Neighborhood Council

AN ORGANIZATION may be analyzed from many vantage points. For example, it is possible to describe a council in terms of the social attitudes of participants to show that people with certain attitudes join councils. However, once this factor has been established, those who wish to recruit members for a council are still faced with the problem of either finding persons with suitable attitudes or transforming people's attitudes into those related to council membership. Neither task is easy to accomplish. Thus analysis from this vantage point contributes little to the practical knowledge of how to recruit members. Although the approach to councils suggested in this chapter and explored in the remainder of the text is not the only way to describe council activities, it is one that has practical implications for the practice of community organization.

The field of community organization is in need of operable concepts that will serve as guidelines for action. Although a good part of this study points up the limitations of traditional explanations of council processes, which emphasize the rational and cognitive in organizational functioning, the intent here is not to deny that these processes occur but to demonstrate that there are others, which may be of equal or greater significance, going on.

Community-Organization Process: The Traditional View

There is general agreement that Murray Ross has most clearly articulated what has been termed *community-organization process.*[1] In his scheme process, or the means by which goals are attained, is, first, problem-solving that moves from definition of the problem, to an explanation of its nature, scope, and implications; to establishing a plan of action for its solution; to taking action. Secondly, it is a process of community integration in which individuals and groups, by participating, develop the skills and capacities necessary for the solution of community problems. The essential difference between the community-organization process and a rational problem-solving process is that the intent of the former is for the community to be better equipped at any stage than at some previous one—or before the process was begun—to identify and deal cooperatively and skillfully with its common problems. In this view a council is part school and part town meeting.

Kahn has noted that the assumption of many process-oriented practitioners is that if a council, such as Du Pont, fails in a particular project, it is because the process was not adequately followed.[2] The contention that factors other than lack of adherence to process intervene in a council's success or failure has been the subject of a good deal of professional discourse in recent years. These criticisms as well as those of process itself may be summarized as follows:

Locus of Decision-making

Community-organization process is concerned with solving community problems through a process that takes place primarily within the confines of an organization. However, a neighborhood in which a council is situated may solve its problems by means of any number of processes, from informal discussions among family heads or people of high status, to behind-the-scenes negotiation by politicians, or even to decisions by referendum and vote. Any attempt to change the way decisions have been made will in most neighborhoods engender considerable conflict and resistance.

The desire to bring together into the council all elements of a neighborhood makes a process-oriented council likely to regard all projects as equally valuable as long as members desire to work on them. The rationalization is that as long as the process is adhered to, attitudes and values that ultimately will lead to the desired changes are being developed. Thus, the council often chooses uncontroversial projects that have little effect on the substructures of neighborhoods and almost no effect on attitudes and values, for example, cleanup campaigns, health examinations, and park beautification. Ultimately such projects lead individuals to question the importance of the council's work.

Rationalism

The ideal process assumes a high degree of rationalism and orderliness on the part of the council so that it can move sequentially from one subprocess to another, that is, from identifying community needs, to setting priorities, to procuring resources, etc. However, in a situation of conflicting interests, values, and attitudes, which is common to most councils, there are severe limitations on the degree of orderliness and rationalism that can be followed. Conceivably, the council's ability to procure resources for a particular project would have considerable effect on the priority assigned to that project as opposed to a project of equal importance for which there was no expectation of procuring resources. There is little reason to assume that the subprocesses go on independently of one another. More likely, they affect one another and thus change the way process works in actual practice.

Overgeneralization

The ideal process sets forth a way of solving community problems that is quite general. It excludes or merely alludes to a number of variables that impinge on the solution of problems. Although it asserts that problems must be studied and analyzed, it does not help to isolate the crucial variables involved in any specific problem. The simple procedural statement that diagnosis of problems must take place is not enough. Without substantive knowledge of how to handle specific problem areas, such as how one improves race relations, these problems cannot be solved.

Organizational Perspective

The process orientation includes a limited view of organizational functioning. A project that is good for the neighborhood is assumed to be good for the council and vice versa. Yet racial integration, although conceivably good for the neighborhood, might destroy a council if it provokes great internal conflict. Because of a council's financial state, it may be forced to sponsor projects that involve little expenditure of money, when what the neighborhood needs is projects requiring a considerable expenditure.

Not part of the process orientation is the view that an organization leads a life of its own dictated by its need for survival and the diverse interests and desires of its members and that these needs and desires may considerably alter the goals and procedures of the organization. Failure to consider these facts has often resulted in councils' pursuing unrealistic goals and strategies, such as the adoption of long-range projects when there is no way to maintain the organization in the short run. It has also resulted in councils' neglecting to perceive and deal with goal displacements, for example, when they become coffee klatches.

In addition to an overformalized view of a council as having a fixed structure of committees and offices through which the various subprocesses take place, the process orientation implies an idealized view of citizens and neighborhoods. It assumes that people have an infinite capacity to change and choose wisely in the management of their affairs, that communities are essentially unstratified and not composed of conflicting subgroups, and that knowledge will lead not only to action but to rational action.

The Exchange Process

Partly because of these criticisms of process, many social workers have questioned the utility of neighborhood councils. Mobilization for Youth and similar community-action organizations around the country have been based on the premise that council structures on a small or a large scale are not adequate for solving present-day social problems. Morris and Rein state the case succinctly:

These new approaches are characterized by the following elements: they are partisan rather than federated; their influences are derived from non-local rather than local sources; they are likely to be public rather than voluntary; they are concerned with political skills more than they are with consensus forming skills; and their goal is change in the community structure rather than coordination of available resources.[3]

Implicit in much of the criticism is the assumption that councils inevitably operate according to the rhetoric of process. Many no doubt do. Du Pont did not, as the recounting of its activities will show.

In this study the focus of analysis is on social exchange. According to Blau, this type of exchange refers to individuals' voluntary actions that are motivated by the returns they are expected to bring.[4] There is a body of opinion, articulated first by George Homans, that social behavior can be conceived as a form of exchange.[5] These exchanges may occur between individuals, groups, or organizations. Exchange means that something is invested in human relationships in the hope of some return or reward. A council is thus one of the possible locales for exchange. Viewed in this light, the mode of analysis of a council shifts from the traditional community-organization process to an exchange process. As such a council is as much a market as it is a school and town meeting.

Resources

A primary element of the exchange process in the neighborhood council is the resources that that council needs. It must get these from individuals or other organizations in exchange for the rewards it produces. Dahl has suggested some of the resources a council might need: "an individual's time; access to money, credit, wealth; control over jobs; control over information; esteem or social standing; the possession of charisma, popularity, legitimacy, legality. . . . The list might also include solidarity: the capacity of a member of society to evoke support from others . . . intelligence, education, and perhaps even one's energy level."[6]

The possession of such resources enables a council to utilize them for the achievement of goals. However, resources are necessary to maintain a council as well as to achieve its goals.[7] Etzioni notes that although organizations must devote part of their resources to achieving goals, they have to devote other resources, not only to the recruitment of further resources to attain goals but also to the maintenance of units performing service activities, for example, the development of morale or good public relations.

Rewards and Costs

A second critical element that should be examined in the exchange process is the rewards at a council's disposal that individuals and other organizations seek. It can be surmised that just as in a business where the need for money exerts a dominant influence on the way the business operates, so in a council the need for rewards exerts a similar dominant influence.

A reward may be defined as anything to which someone or some organization ascribes value, be it a thing, an emotion, or an idea. In other words, a reward can be money, prestige, or fulfillment of an abstract desire, such as to be a good Christian or a good citizen. For purposes of this study, rewards are classified in four ways:

1. Rewards of a primarily emotional nature (friendship, praise, self-esteem)
2. Rewards engendered by services that the council produces (a new school, more police protection)

3. Rewards that satisfy one's ideological commitments, such as being a good American or a good Christian
4. Rewards that have negotiable value in systems other than the council, such as getting oneself in the public eye or enhancing the prestige of one's church or ethnic group

These will be referred to as follows: (1) emotional rewards, (2) service rewards, (3) ideological rewards, and (4) negotiable rewards.[8]

If Homan's formulation is applied, a participant in a council may be thought to invest his time, money, skill, etc., in exchange for some output or reward. He puts in something in the expectation of getting something out. Just like a person investing money in a business, the investor in a council must calculate the possible risks of his involvement and the potential rewards of investing his resources in other places.[9] These risks and forgone potentialities become the cost of his participation. Cost refers to those risks, obligations, undesired consequences, and lost opportunities which are incurred in securing social rewards and detract from the value of the reward.

In a council these costs may range from not wanting to be associated with certain people, to losing time with family, to not wanting to associate with futile causes, etc. Like rewards, costs may also be classified as to their nature—emotional, service, ideological, negotiable. Therefore, any reward a participant receives is potentially offset by the costs incurred in participating.

To get a true picture of the rewards that accrue to a participant one must realize that each individual has more than one status. A man is at the same time father, doctor, Jew, neighbor, husband, Rotarian, etc. Conceivably a reward may be salient in one status but costly in others, salient in many but costly in one, etc. For example, a local merchant who is an officer of the council may lose business if the council engages in controversial activities. A mother who devotes great amounts of time to the council may incur considerable costs as a wife. The fact that each person is a multi-status individual and that one status may conflict with another makes the production of rewards a difficult task. Furthermore, since there is a level of council rewards that goes directly to other organizations, conflict among organizations also limits a council's ability to produce rewards.

Production of rewards. In general, councils produce rewards in one or more of three ways: (1) by achieving specific goals, (2) through the procedures by which these goals are achieved, or (3) through structural devices, such as formal offices or informal cliques. Rewards pro-

duced by councils may go to individuals or to organizations or to some
combination of both. It can be hypothesized that the quantity and
quality of rewards available in a council may be varied by manipulating its goals, procedures, or structure.

The reward potential of any council goal can be determined by
evaluating its rewards and costs to individual participants in their multiple statuses and to organizations in their interrelationships. Although
a council goal, such as a new school, may be potentially rewarding, the
procedures the council intends to use in pursuing the project may be
extremely costly, for example, boycotting the present school. Therefore,
any procedure the council contemplates using must be analyzed in terms
of its potential rewards and costs to individuals and organizations.

Similarly, a project may be rewarding to all individuals and organizations in the neighborhood, and the procedures the council expects to
engage in may also be rewarding, but the structure of the council may
lead participants to feel that participation is too costly and nonrewarding. Formal offices may be filled by people with whom others do not
wish to associate, or past projects of a council may make people feel
that the council is a worthless organization. Therefore, the structure of
the council must also be analyzed in terms of the rewards and costs it
produces for individuals and organizations.

To create exchanges for the resources it needs, a neighborhood
council can raise rewards and lower costs by manipulating its goals,
procedures, and structure. A council's ability to lower costs deserves
emphasis, for it is easily overlooked. One of the major reasons participants may have for joining an organization is to lower their costs in
order to achieve a goal. A settlement house, for instance, may join a
council so it can provide particular kinds of activities for its members
in cooperation with other organizations. Although many reasons may
motivate this cooperation, one certainly is that the same program
attempted alone would involve a larger outlay of money and staff time.
Thus, by participating in the council program, the settlement lowers
its costs considerably.

The use and distribution of rewards.   Traditional thinking has over-
simplified the uses to which rewards may be put and the way in which
they are distributed. The usual assumption is that rewards accrue to
participants either by working on or by achieving a particular project.
However, the attaining of rewards does not always occur immediately
or directly. For example, the long-term nature of some projects so
raises their costs that no matter how many rewards were initially con-

nected with them, the projects can no longer be considered a source of reward. Similarly, when a project is unsuccessful, participants are thought to receive very few rewards and other projects are sought to provide rewards. In actuality, it may be possible for councils to develop techniques whereby such potentially costly activities can be turned into sources of reward.

Council survival may be related to its ability to develop mechanisms for the storing and distribution of rewards that may be used during periods of project stalemate and failure. This capacity requires thinking of rewards and costs not only in relationship to participants but to the council itself. Rewards do not automatically accrue to the council from its activities. Some projects and procedures can be rewarding to a small number of participants but not to the council itself. No one in the neighborhood outside of a small number of participants may know that the council was responsible for having a guard posted at a school crossing or for rehabilitating a park. Therefore, the council must develop ways of turning these projects into sources of reward for its future use.

One important way is for a council to carry out its projects so that commitment to itself as an organization and solidarity among its members are developed. Once this commitment and solidarity have been developed, a new source of rewards has actually been generated because commitment and solidarity, once developed in a member, can act as self-rewarding mechanisms. As such, they can give a council a stable source of rewards and free it from the instabilities of complete dependence on successful projects as its major source of rewards.

Rewards serve other uses for councils than mere inducements for individual participation. They play a vital part in goal achievement. A great deal of what councils do may be characterized as attempts to influence people and organizations in certain directions. Traditionally, in social work council influence has been conceived as the outcome of a dispassionate discussion based on a clear understanding of all the facts. What generally has not been stressed is that people are also influenced, apart from their own judgment of a situation, by others who have the ability to confer or withhold rewards. This type of influence is as vital to neighborhood councils as rational thinking and persuasion.

Without a supply of rewards, councils are limited in their ability to develop influence. Council structure, procedures, and goals must be analyzed in terms of the rewards and costs they bring to the organization itself. These rewards and costs provide the base upon which influence can be built.

Limitations of the Exchange Model

An exchange model cannot explain all aspects of council functioning. It is not a substitute for the substantive knowledge of how to organize a Little League or how to run a meeting or how to develop an urban renewal plan. In addition, many of the problems inherent in making the model more operable are beyond the scope of this study, for example, the relationships among the various classifications of rewards, the manner in which rates of exchange are established, and the processes that participants go through in the selection of rewards. Nor does the exchange model assume that participants are aware of all rewards and act rationally and solely on a reward-seeking basis. Blau emphatically makes this point in defending his emphasis on the exchange process in the analysis of interaction:

What is explicitly not assumed here is that men have complete information, that they have no social commitments restricting their alternatives, that their preferences are entirely consistent or remain constant, or that they pursue one specific ultimate goal to the exclusion of all other. . . . The only assumption made is that human beings choose alternative potential associates or courses of action by evaluating the experiences or expected experiences with each in terms of a preference ranking and then selecting the best alternative.[10]

A great many concepts other than exchange are used in this study to explain the functioning of Du Pont, for example, role, reference group, and power. Their use has been necessary because, as noted, a theory of exchange does not illuminate all aspects of council functioning. Yet, it must be pointed out that none of the other existing concepts accomplish this end either.

It may legitimately be asked, Why focus on exchange when other concepts such as power and influence to an extent include the concept of exchange and in some ways have been more adequately conceptualized? There are a number of reasons: First, if this were to be solely a study of how Du Pont achieved its goals, then a focus on power would have been relevant. This concept has been used most often in case studies of political action and goal attainment. However, in this study not only are problems of organizational goal attainment considered but also problems of organizational maintenance. How to get the corner butcher into the council and how to keep him participating once he is there are matters of no small concern. The concept of power is not really adequate for this level of problem. Power relations and organizational maintenance are both viewed by Blau in the context of exchange. Thus, his concept offers a way of understanding these dual organizational needs.

Secondly, influence can be developed through the use of techniques other than exchange, for example, persuasion, deception, and coercion. Traditionally, as noted, social work has emphasized rational persuasion in its discussion of influence techniques. Other techniques have been considered somewhat illegitimate. The decision to emphasize exchange was specifically made to point out the fact through the analysis of Du Pont's activities that even when decisions seemed to be made solely on the basis of rationality or process, a great deal of exchange was also taking place.

Thirdly and most importantly, staff workers must be able to understand the effect of their own actions, as well as those of the council, on the neighborhood and on the council itself. Perhaps the chief utility of an exchange model is that it links council and neighborhood, individual and organization, person and group. The skill of a community organizer rests considerably on his ability to manipulate an organization's structure and procedures to achieve its ends. The worker requires some integrative concept by which he can gauge the effect of these manipulations on the council, its participants, and its overall goals. Translating the results and expected results of his actions into rewards and costs fulfills this need. A council is more than its supply of rewards, more than the way these rewards are produced and exchanged, just as a neighborhood's social structure includes more than the manner in which rewards and resources are exchanged and allocated. Yet in both cases the exchange processes are such a central function that a great deal can be learned about how council and neighborhood operate, separately and together, by understanding these processes.

For example, if a council were to want to secure improvements in a park, an analysis of the goal of park improvement itself and the possible ways of getting the improvements made (in terms of the rewards and costs that would accrue to the council) would make it possible to judge the effects of this project on the council. Does the project increase the council's influence or prestige? What resources at the council's disposal will it have to commit? Once a project's effect on the council has been estimated, it is then important to understand how the project will affect the neighborhood. How will the distribution of rewards in the neighborhood be affected by the way the council goes about improving the park and by the project itself? Who receives the rewards offered? Do these factors change the balance or tip the scales in favor of one group or another? Who loses prestige? Who gains it?

Is the neighborhood's supply of resources overcommitted? Has the control over certain rewards actually been changed?

Likewise, analytic questions can be asked about individuals: why do some join and not others? What is the significance of people not completing their tasks? How can they be induced to complete them? What is the effect of the executive committee's making all the decisions? Staff workers need some conceptual way to think about these organizational problems that is related to individual functioning and interaction. In a profession such as social work, where the ultimate test of utility must be the effect of its actions on individuals, it is crucial to have a theoretical way to explain the interrelationships of individuals and organizations such as councils. The exchange model fulfills this professional need, for it enables a worker to relate an individual's actions to organizational actions and vice versa.

Summary

Although many books have been written about community organization and attention has been given to community-organization workers, their techniques, and their methods, considerably less emphasis has been given to the functioning of organizations, such as councils, in which community organizers work. Knowledge about how such organizations operate is important for anyone interested in using or understanding how they function as instruments of community betterment and control.

The intent of this study is to explore those insights which the exchange model at its present level of sophistication brings to the understanding of community affairs. The analyses begin with a detailed discussion of the events surrounding the founding of the Du Pont Neighborhood Council.

NOTES

1. Ross defines process as "a sequential series of events which progresses from the identification of needs or objectives, to ordering and ranking the needs or objectives, and then to developing the confidence and will to work on them, finding the resources internal and external, to deal with them, taking action in respect to them, and in so doing extends and develops cooperative and collaborative attitudes and practices in the community." Murray G. Ross, *Community Organization* (New York: Harper and Bros., 1955), p. 39. Hence-

forth *community-organization process* may also be referred to as *process*.
2. Alfred J. Kahn, "Social Science and the Conceptual Framework for Community Organization Research," *Social Science Theory and Social Work Research*, ed. Leonard S. Kogan (New York: National Association of Social Workers, 1960), p. 76.
3. Robert Morris and Martin Rein, "Emerging Patterns in Community Planning," *Social Welfare Practice, 1963* (New York: Columbia University Press, 1963), p. 168.
4. Social exchange differs in important ways from strictly economic exchange. The basic and most crucial distinction is that social exchange entails unspecified obligations. See Peter M. Blau, *Exchange and Power in Social Life* (New York: John Wiley & Sons, 1964), p. 61.
5. George C. Homans, "Social Behavior as Exchange," *American Journal of Sociology*, LXIII (May 1958).
6. Robert A. Dahl, *Who Governs: Democracy and Power in an American City* (New Haven: Yale University Press, 1961), p. 226.
7. The systems model of organizational analysis is used throughout this study. Amitai Etzioni distinguishes between the systems and the goal model in "Two Approaches to Organizational Analysis: A Critique and a Suggestion," *Administrative Science Quarterly*, V (September 1960), 259.
8. No contention is offered that this is the only way of classifying rewards or that the four categories are mutually exclusive. It is contended, however, that the categories provide sufficient discrimination to be analytically fruitful. For a three-type classification of rewards, see Peter B. Clark and James Q. Wilson, "Incentive Systems," *Administrative Science Quarterly*, VI (September 1961).
9. The concept of rewards in relation to organizational functioning was first emphasized by Chester I. Barnard, *The Functions of the Executive* (Cambridge: Harvard University Press, 1938), pp. 57–61. It was further expanded by James G. March and Herbert A. Simon, "The Theory of Organizational Equilibrium," *Complex Organizations*, ed. Amitai Etzioni (New York: Holt, Rinehart and Winston, 1961), pp. 61–71, and John W. Thibaut and Harold H. Kelley, *The Social Psychology of Groups* (New York: John Wiley & Sons, 1959), pp. 31–50. A major development of the concept, relating it to an exchange process has been accomplished by Blau, *Exchange and Power*. Although the concept has its roots in Hobbes and the classical economists and has been adopted by modern-day game theorists, the exchange concept differs from the older concept in one crucial aspect. It admits that actors will evaluate their exchanges from many vantage points other than strictly economics, power, or the desire to win, and that one cannot always predict the relative weights assigned to exchanges. Granting this limitation, see p. 24 of this text for Blau's defense of the utility of the concept.
10. Blau, *Exchange and Power*, p. 18. For a thorough analysis and critique of Blau's concept of exchange, see S. N. Eisenstadt, "Review of Exchange and Power in Social Life," *American Journal of Sociology*, LXXI (November 1965), 333–34.

Part II

Du Pont's Exchanges

3

Crisis, Coalition, and Character

THERE IS a similarity in the early life of a considerable number of councils. The usual pattern is for a council to come into existence during a time of community crisis. It could be a physical disaster or a social one, such as a child being run over or a woman molested. The whole community is concerned. A settlement house or similar organization issues a call for a community meeting, and all groups in the community, as well as interested individuals, are invited.

Generally, a committee formed to deal with such a crisis receives a good deal of support, and in many cases its efforts are successful. While positive feeling is strong, someone frequently suggests that many other things in the community need improvement—schools, garbage collection, police protection, recreational facilities, housing, and the like. It is at this point that a council is formed. Officers are elected, a constitution is framed, and committee chairmen are selected. Although enthusiasm may at first be high, often trouble, signaled by a drop-off in attendance, soon becomes apparent.

At this stage of development a typical council experience might read as follows:[1] The chairman of the education committee calls her second meeting, and only her friends and one or two others attend. At a general membership meeting about police protection, there is a small turnout—the officers of the organization, a few invited guests, and a handful of neighborhood cranks. The council struggles on for a period

of months. Summer arrives, creating a natural lull as people attend to
their vacations. In the fall there is a burst of enthusiasm, usually centered around the election of a new slate of officers, who are elected
with high hopes and a call for citizen participation. This activity seldom materializes, and soon afterward the council disintegrates.

A major organizational function that a crisis performs for a council
is the offering of a source of highly salient rewards and costs to potential participants. A crisis inherently is a threat and, therefore, its solution is potentially rewarding. In addition, in many crisis situations,
because there is no preexisting way to deal with the emergency, a
council can enlist the support of the total community. Participants cannot invest their resources in other organizations to receive the rewards
that resolving the crisis would give them.

Given the common experience of councils evolving out of crises, it
can be hypothesized that crises perform certain organizational functions and that the end of the crisis does not mean that these functions
no longer need to be performed. A substitute has to be found to carry
on the functions that the crisis performed. The problem of finding substitute sources of reward as crises are resolved is immense. Most projects of a noncrisis nature are nowhere as potentially rewarding to
participants as projects associated with crises. Getting a new park is
seldom as salient a reward for a potential participant as making sure
that his teen-ager is not killed on the way home from school or church.
In addition, in a crisis situation the cost of participation is compensated
by the potential rewards from crisis resolution. In a noncrisis situation
the rewards available can seldom overcome the costs, which include
such sentiments as, "I don't want to associate with the people in the
council" or "I'd rather play golf." There is also the recourse of return-
ing to already existing methods of dealing with routine community
problems.

Part of the reason Du Pont did not face the usual early death of other
councils lies in the nature of the crises it faced. Teen-age gang warfare
did not subside for several years after the council's birth. Interracial
tension never did die out. The schools remained a problem. Although
Du Pont ultimately, as will be shown, had to find alternative sources
of reward, the lingering nature of the crises made the job somewhat
easier because a source of rewards was still available. Nevertheless, in
many neighborhoods crises linger on, but the council does not survive.
It may be, then, that the way in which Du Pont dealt with its initiating
crisis accounts for its survival.

Crisis

Violence took several forms among Du Pont's teen-agers. The Sports-
men, a group of Negro boys living outside Du Pont, began raiding
Jones Housing Project and beating up members of a group called the
Jones Boys. The battle lines, which determined who was going to control the "turf," were similar to those drawn all over the city. The constant fights, knifings, and vandalism wrought by these gang conflicts
greatly alarmed the Italian community, whose dream of a quiet,
friendly, refuge from the hustle and bustle of the city was shaken.

At this time there were groups of young Italian men, mostly unem-
ployed, hanging out in storefront social clubs, who took it upon
themselves to defend the Italian community. A sign in one storefront
read: "No Niggers, Spiks or Kikes on Doctrine Street." These groups
were so successful in their campaign that a neighborhood pattern
developed whereby Negroes and Puerto Ricans avoided Doctrine
Street and used Harold Street instead when on the way to and from the
Jones Housing Project. When Jewish teen-agers began to be harassed
and "shook down," the total community was involved.[2]

In such a crisis situation the need to explain and blame is evident.
The Italians tended to view themselves as under attack, asking angrily,
"Why don't the Protestant missions control their kids?" The Jews saw
in the Italian community Fascist elements that were provoking the
attacks on their children; the Negroes and the Puerto Ricans traced
the problem to prejudice; and the Protestants accused the Catholic
churches of not assuming responsibility for their own.

The reaction of the Du Pont Council was twofold: it formed a public
safety committee, comprised mainly of Jewish parents concerned about
the attacks on their children. This group viewed the Italian community
as the source of their problems and took a vigilante approach, crying,
"Get more police protection and form a safety association that will
help the police." The social work staff workers who advised this committee sought to analyze the problem as a lack of services, such as recreation and employment for teen-agers and the neighborhood. Gradually a
shift occurred from the vigilante approach to an effort aimed at getting
parents and organizations to take responsibility for the teen-agers.
Visits were made to parents of the most notorious teen-agers. The site
of the Du Pont meetings rotated among the local organizations.

Items in the *Du Pont News* in early 1957 illustrate this shift:

The police are doing their part. . . . The only ones who could be doing more
to help are parents and friends of the youths responsible for this violence.

Prejudice and attempts to protect their own will not help the situation.[3]

Other work of the Public Safety Committee has resulted in the installation of new street lights on Cherry Street between Catherine and Market Streets. The committee has also met with a Park Department representative to inquire about facilities in the neighborhood and found that Cherry Street Gym can accommodate teams and groups from neighborhood churches and centers in addition to its regular users.[4]

In addition to the public safety committee, Du Pont formed a youth team known in the neighborhood as the rumbles committee. This group was made up of paid staff representatives of local organizations that worked with teen-agers—churches, social agencies, police, schools, parks. Only the Italian Catholic organizations did not participate. The function of this committee was to coordinate the activities of all organizations in order to stop the violence.

There was recognition that no one group could solve the problems. The Protestant missions, the schools, and the police were under heavy criticism for not being able to deal with the Negro and Puerto Rican teen-agers.[5] In addition, these organizations felt threatened by the vigilante approach that was spreading through the neighborhood. The unifying feeling was that professionals should handle certain situations.[6]

The professional rumbles committee worked out an elaborate twenty-four-hour communications network; and during the turbulent years in Du Pont, it succeeded in breaking up many potentially violent situations. In one instance hundreds of whites lined up on the opposite side of the street from as many Negroes and Puerto Ricans, with the rumbles committee and other local citizens in the middle—and the clash was averted. In addition to blocking violence, the committee took the coordination and improvement of local services as one of its goals. A summer program for teen-agers was planned for the entire neighborhood, with several agencies sharing resources. Confidential information about families and teen-agers was shared, and responsibilities for various situations and individuals were assigned to different organizations.[7]

Exchanges

Certain groups and individuals were able to procure rewards from the council and others were not. A pattern of exchanges is discernible in Du Pont's early responses to gang warfare and violence. These exchange patterns had a great effect on Du Pont and merit close examination.[8]

Exchanges with individuals. There have been countless attempts with little success to coordinate social agencies in delinquency control.[9]

Rumbles committees formed in other sections of HEED were never so successful as in Du Pont. To some extent success can be attributed to the high ideological commitment to citizen participation of the directors of three local agencies. They had a wide range of resources to put at the council's disposal.

Not the least of the resources these men possessed were their own talents. Father James Gone of the Episcopal mission has since left the community to head a national program for training Episcopal ministers to work with inner-city youth. Reverend John Older of the Baptists edited a national Baptist journal, had written two books on the church and urban affairs, and was known as a man with great administrative capacity. The director of Jefferson House, Mr. George Smitz, was perhaps the strongest advocate of neighborhood councils of the three. He felt that, as a staff worker, he could organize a successful neighborhood council in any neighborhood if he were given the opportunity. All three of these men received ideological rewards from their participation.

The council committees concerned with delinquency provided tangible service and emotional rewards to individuals in their ethnic status. The concerns of Negroes and Puerto Ricans about prejudice and lack of services were given a voice. Instead of being a mass of people with no outlet, they had a forum with powerful spokesmen and resources. An editorial in the first issue of the *Du Pont News*, published in February 1957, voiced this view of the council. The old neighborhood newspaper, put out in the middle- and low-income projects by a predominantly Jewish staff, officially went out of business at this time and turned over to Du Pont what little resources it had. A member of the retiring staff wrote:

During the past year and up to its last issue [November 2, 1956], the staff of the *TV-Jones News* has been following the activities of the Du Pont Neighborhood Council with growing interest. We realized increasingly that Du Pont was a new and vital force in the community, more capable of answering and reflecting its needs than we. . . . For this reason the . . . Executive Board of the TV T.A. and the Jones T.A. voted to have the Du Pont Neighborhood Council take over the News.[10]

The reason for the turnover is not difficult to understand. Safety on the streets was a major concern of the Jewish group. The involvement of Jews in the public safety committee tended to give Jews in the area the feeling that the council would deal with this problem appropriately. Their liberal traditions required that their concern for safety not be expressed in an anti-Negro and Puerto Rican bias.

Exchanges with organizations. Not only did Rev. Mr. Older, Rev. Mr. Gone, and Mr. Smitz receive personal ideological rewards for their support of Du Pont, but they obtained rewards that enhanced their organizations as well. Mr. Smitz's situation in 1957 is indicative of how organizations received rewards from Du Pont. Traditionally Jefferson House had been an Italian-oriented institution. When large numbers of Negroes and Puerto Ricans flocked into the neighborhood, the director felt that they had a right to service from his agency, and he began to promote a policy of racial balance. Some Italian teen-agers, resenting Negroes and Puerto Ricans coming to the house, which they viewed as their own, instituted a policy of harassment to let the Negroes and Puerto Ricans know that they were not wanted. They had sufficient success to make Mr. Smitz feel that the house was isolated from the Negro and Puerto Rican teen-agers he wanted to reach. However, the organization of the rumbles committee gave him an opportunity to make contact with these teen-agers. Since the Protestant ministers felt "the more services the better," they were willing to send their teen-agers to the house as well as to help stop the harassment of Negroes and Puerto Ricans by Italians. Thus, in 1956–1957 a pattern of exchanges between the Protestant missions and Jefferson House was developed through working together in the rumbles committee. This exchange pattern has been continued throughout Du Pont down through the years.

The manner in which social problems are defined can be one of the major rewards a council has to give to an organization. Although delinquency can be defined in terms of police laxity or parental laxity, etc., the public safety committee and the rumbles committee tended to relate delinquency to prejudice and a lack of services. The plea for more services was close to the hearts of the social agencies, and they could point to increasing delinquency as a need for more money and staff. Thus this orientation enhanced their organizational ends.

The *Du Pont News* article concerning prejudice was referring to the Italian Catholics, since Negroes, Puerto Ricans, and Jews are generally referred to as the recipients of prejudice.[11] The lack of Italian representation on the public safety and rumbles committees is important to understand, for it made possible the definition of delinquency that the Roman Catholic groups would have most resisted. The position toward delinquency of the Italian Catholic churches in Du Pont in the middle 1950s is best understood in terms of their attitude toward authority. The churches had certain rules and regulations. If people did not conform, they were simply out of the church. Thus the attitude of the priests toward delinquency was in terms of individuals breaking rules and regulations. They said: "Lawbreakers should be excluded from the community. It is the job of the police to do this."[12] The idea that a lack of services, prejudice, or segregation caused delinquency did not conform to the churches' belief in the individual's responsibility for his own acts. The definition of delinquency adopted by Du Pont not only failed to provide rewards to the Roman Catholic organizations but imputed to these organizations a lack of civic-mindedness and un-Americanism. Instead of supplying rewards, Du Pont was actually imposing costs on them.

Effects of the Exchanges

On a quiet fall evening in 1963, the rumor suddenly spread through the Italian community that an Italian boy had been kidnapped by a group of Negroes. A mob gathered in front of one of the Italian churches, and the elderly priest had a difficult time getting it to disperse, even after it was found that the boy had merely played hookey from school and had been afraid to go home. The following day members of the local agencies met, including the elderly priest, who had always been disinterested in the council, to discuss ways of reactivating the rumbles committee to deal with such situations.

The Neighborhood

The significance of this chain of events was that the council was looked to by all segments of the community as the group best suited to deal with this type of situation. Clearly, the neighborhood social system had been altered to the extent that at least one problem—racial outbreaks—had become the province of the council. As Reitzes notes, "In modern mass society the basis for individual behavior in situations of racial contacts becomes increasingly the definition of the situation provided to the individual by deliberately organized collectives. This organizational structuring is effective to the extent that it defines the situation for the individual in terms of his specific interest in the situation."[13]

The public safety and rumbles committees helped to achieve the desired ends of the Du Pont Council: violence and vandalism were reduced, and a stable pattern of exchanges was established between certain groups and organizations to ensure the continued survival of the council. However, the consequences of these committee actions were not all positive. Du Pont paid a price as an organization.

The Council

The importance of analyzing an organization's public image to determine its usefulness in attaining the organization's goals has been clearly stated by Selznick. He uses the word *character* rather than *image*, but his meaning is clear:

The character of an organization is the product of its ingrained methods of work, its natural allies, its stake in the course of events, the predispositions of its personnel, and the labels (deserved and undeserved) which have become attached to it. These characteristics reflect the organization's controlling roles and purposes; they generate those established patterns of expectation with which the organization is uniquely identified. These expectations put real limits on the functioning and capabilities of an organization, and often may dictate the death of an organization and the formation of a new one if certain goals are to be accomplished.[14]

Labels.   Certain labels became attached to Du Pont. In its first year the council president was the director of Jefferson House, and so most of the council business was conducted at and through Jefferson House. It was inevitable that the neighborhood should tend to confuse the council with the house. Some of the council's later difficulties with the Italian community no doubt stemmed from this association.

As noted, Jefferson House was once an Italian-oriented settlement. When the house moved into its new quarters in the Jones Housing Project, the director pursued a policy of quotas between whites and Negroes. Gradually the Italian community withdrew from the settlement, which it defined as a Negro and Puerto Rican organization. When the director permitted the Episcopalians to conduct a Sunday school in the settlement, the house's status in the Italian community reached a low ebb. The natural alliance between the settlement and the Protestant churches was clear to all. Besides, the activity of the Protestant clergy in the rumbles committee left no doubt that the values they stood for, such as racial integration, would be dominant. Given this situation, the wariness of the Italian community seems understandable.

Style of operation.   The chairman of the public safety committee was a probation officer. The members of the rumbles committee were all paid community workers. Committee work was often long and tedious, requiring organizational skill, verbal sophistication, understanding of other points of view, and the ability to wait—qualities not generally related to the working class. Thus the image that Du Pont presented could not have been very positive for members of this class.[15] Its membership was middle class in orientation. Much of its work involved negotiation with other organizations and agencies, local and citywide, and, therefore, required a good deal of knowledge and ability on the part of the negotiators. When work was to be done in the committees, if enough people did not volunteer, there was always the staff worker. In addition, to help the worker, there were the staffs of the settlement house and the missions.

The Du Pont neighborhood was almost two-thirds Roman Catholic. However, the council's natural allies were the Protestants. Shortly after the council's inception, it was dependent on Jefferson House and the Protestant churches for a considerable part of its needed resources of money, facilities, and commitment. In addition, the neighborhood was 90 percent working class. However, honorific offices were open only to those possessing skills associated with middle-class professionalism. The council's goals—such as broadening the community's health services, expanding school facilities, developing urban renewal, improving civic services—did not until the late sixties have priority with the working class. Nor are such patterns as fact-finding, committee deliberations, and formal group discussions akin to working-class patterns. Thus the fact that Du Pont never developed a mass following in the neighborhood is consistent with its initial image as a Protestant, middle-class organization.

Coalition. As a result of their experience in the rumbles committee, the directors of the Protestant missions and the settlement house became aware that they shared similar interests and goals for the neighborhood in such matters as housing, schools, health, and recreation. It was apparent that by combining their resources in the council, they would have an organizational tool with which they could exert considerable influence on the neighborhood. Their coalition, joined with the liberal Jewish elements, made them a powerful factor to offset the strength of the only other organizations of consequence, the Catholic churches and the regular Democratic and Republican clubs.[16]

The rumbles committee and the public safety committee established a pattern for council relationships with the Roman Catholics and the regular political organizations. A member of the council explained its tactics regarding these organizations as follows: "Always attempt to involve them; short of this, define problems in such a manner that their outright opposition is muted or neutralized and then, if at all possible, go ahead on our own."

The durability of this basic council tactic, as well as the coalition itself, was evidenced by the council's civil rights activities in 1963. The Italian organizations had never demonstrated much concern for the rights of Negroes. Although there had been constant concern in Du Pont lest the council antagonize the Italian groups to the point that they would break completely with the council, this concern did not affect the council's thinking in relation to the 1963 march on Washington.[17] At an executive meeting Mr. A. of HEED presented plans for the march on Washington and asked the council to participate. There was some disagreement about what the council should do. Mr. L. felt that the council should not give its full support but should urge its members to paticipate as individuals. He commented that many of the organizations were not represented at this meeting and should be allowed to vote on the issue. However, the majority of the executive committee felt that it was necessary for the council to participate, that they might get some criticism, but that they should accept this risk because the issue was so vital to the area and to the country as a whole.

The council participated as an organization by setting up registration tables in front of the settlement and later by voting one hundred dollars to further the march on Washington. The regular political clubs and the Catholic churches did not protest; nor did they actively participate. Their overt relationship to the council did not change; nor did they threaten to stop paying their twenty-five-dollar yearly dues, even though part of it went for the one-hundred-dollar donation. Although their opposition had been neutralized, their support had not been gained.

Summary

One way to account for the short life span of most neighborhood councils is to state that a coalition of individuals and groups brought together by a crisis is seldom able, after the crisis is resolved, to find the resources necessary to maintain an organization. Those who pledge resources to the council in times of crisis return to their precrisis commitments—family, social clubs, business, etc. In this vein Blau states:

The establishment of an organization requires capital investments, often in the form of financial investments, always in the form of social investments. Resources and efforts, which could be spent directly to obtain rewards, must be devoted to building the organization and developing its specialized structure, to recruiting members and contributors, to coordinating their activities and instituting normative standards for them to follow. . . . All this entails postponement of gratifications, which requires a surplus of resources beyond those merely sufficient to meet current minimum needs. Hence only individuals or groups with surplus resources can establish a business, organize a union or create a political organization.[18]

Coalitions are not easy to maintain.[19] Yet if an organization wishes to exert control over a community, it must forge a coalition of interests. As most communities are stratified and heterogeneous, a degree of conflict with those outside the coalition can be anticipated. These conflicts can both destroy a coalition and limit its ability to recruit needed resources.

The facilities, staff, money, organizational expertise, time, and political contacts possessed by Jefferson House and the Protestant missions were the surplus resources that made the establishment of the Du Pont Council possible. Yet, ample as these resources were, they were not sufficient to achieve the goals of the council in such areas as race relations, housing, and politics. Resources necessary for the attainment of these goals rested in groups outside the coalition. Rewards had to be created to be exchanged for these needed resources.

NOTES

1. This pattern occurred in several committees of SECA, a new HEED council observed by the research team for a period of months. In the years prior to the formation of SECA, the 5 Mile Council and the ABC Council, both HEED councils, died following much the same life cycle as described in the text.
2. Of all the groups perhaps the Chinese suffered the most, being the object of repeated muggings and attacks in the Jones Housing Project. Yet their response was to withdraw more and more to themselves.
3. *Du Pont News*, March 8, 1957, p. 1.
4. *Du Pont News*, February 8, 1957, p. 3.
5. The Protestant missions in the area are best described as religious settlement houses or social agencies.
6. A professional was defined as any paid employee of a local organization.
7. By 1962 violence had subsided, and this committee no longer functioned on a regular basis.
8. In describing the history of Du Pont in terms of exchanges, no implication that the participants knowingly developed exchanges is intended. Discussions with participants about the reasons for particular council actions clearly indicated that they were not operating with an exchange concept. In a few instances reported in subsequent chapters, certain participants were aware of the exchanges involved in a particular situation, but they did not develop their awareness into a generalized mode of operation.
9. See, for example, William Reid, "Interagency Co-ordination in Delinquency Prevention and Control," *Social Service Review*, XXXVIII (December 1964).
10. *Du Pont News*, February 8, 1957, p. 2.
11. See note 3.
12. This attitude was not necessarily held by all Italians in Du Pont.

13. Dietrich C. Reitzes, "The Role of Organizational Structure: Union vs. Neighborhood in a Tension Situation," *Sociology: The Progress of a Decade*, ed. Seymour Lipset and Neil Smelser (Englewood Cliffs, N.J.: Prentice-Hall, 1961), p. 520.

14. Phillip Selznick, *The Organizational Weapon: A Study of Bolshevik Strategy and Tactics* (New York: McGraw-Hill, 1952), p. 56.

15. For a discussion of this point, see John M. Foskett, "The Influence of Social Participation on Community Programs and Activities," *Community Structure and Analysis*, ed. Marvin Sussman (New York: Thomas Y. Crowell, 1959), pp. 324–25, or Herbert J. Gans, *The Urban Villagers* (New York: Free Press, 1962), pp. 263–69.

16. For a discussion of coalitions and tactics, see James D. Thompson and William J. McEwen, "Organizational Goals and Environment," *Complex Organizations*, ed. Amitai Etzioni (New York: Holt, Rinehart and Winston, 1961), pp. 177–86.

17. The tactics of cooperation and neutralization were not completely without costs to Du Pont. Concerns about segregation in local housing were often muted for fear of engaging in direct conflict with local politicians.

18. Peter M. Blau, *Exchange and Power in Social Life* (New York: John Wiley & Sons, 1964), pp. 214–15.

19. An analysis of why Du Pont's coalition held together will be made in the concluding chapter.

4

Little Leaguers

THE ORGANIZATIONAL dilemma that Du Pont faced after the first year of its existence was serious and perhaps typical of what most councils face. Ideally, a neighborhood council attempts to have all groups in a neighborhood come together and make common cause against common problems. However, after a comparatively short time it becomes apparent that not all groups are interested in participating. Some may be outspokenly hostile. Often those groups which display the least interest are the ones most needed if a council is to achieve its goals.

In Du Pont the cooperation of the Italian Catholic organizations was vital if there was to be any improvement in race relations. Yet it was to this group that the Du Pont Council appeared least appealing. The council was not representing what the Italians conceived to be their interests. Racial integration was not their concern. Nor was improvement of the public schools, for their children went to parochial schools. Besides, the same Protestant ministers who were leaders of the council were actively proselytizing Puerto Rican Catholics in the neighborhood. Thus there was a conflict of interest between the coalition that led Du Pont and the Italian Catholic-dominated organizations.

How to offer rewards to both the Italian and non-Italian groups, to bridge this conflict of interest, was the council's major organizational dilemma. It is doubtful that Du Pont would have been so effective had it not been able to surmount this conflict. It can be speculated that the demise of most neighborhood councils is due to their inability to reconcile inherent conflicts among the needs of various groups. Gouldner writes:

Underlying the "rhetoric of needs" is the assumption that gratifications provided for one group need not conflict with the true requirements of another. In short, the rhetoric of needs assumes that the basic needs of different groups in the community are fundamentally compatible. This, I fear, is a metaphysics which is incapable of empirical verification.[1]

Council failure may also be related to another factor. Form notes: "Community activities and social organizations do not necessarily induce solidarity, cooperation and understanding. Not infrequently they serve to crystallize or exaggerate the differences existing among people. Indeed there is evidence that without such organizations stratification on the community-wide level is not likely to evolve."[2] Thus a council that is dominated by middle-class professionals and operating in the style of the middle class might easily be regarded as a nonrewarding organization by lower-class citizens. It would simply serve to crystallize for them the differences that exist between the lower and middle classes.

Du Pont met the organizational dilemma created by conflicts of interest in two ways. The public safety committee had attracted to the council a small number of middle-class Italians. One of these men, Mr. John Brando, was a local pharmacist who was well known and respected in the Italian community. He was alarmed by the effects of gang violence on his business, for people were afraid to walk the streets at night. It was clear to him that unless the violence stopped, his business was going to suffer even more.

Although Mr. Smitz, director of Jefferson House, was the original chairman of the council, he soon realized—as did the other leaders of Du Pont—that having a professional community worker as chairman was a mistake if the council wanted to enlist citizen participation. With Mr. Smitz as chairman, the council tended to be viewed as an adjunct of Jefferson House, no matter what it did. The decision to ask Mr. Brando to serve as chairman and his acceptance were crucial to the survival and effectiveness of Du Pont.[3] No one in the Italian community ever dreamed of calling Mr. Brando a Communist. The priests knew him to be a good Catholic. Besides the ability of the council to put out the *Du Pont News,* a unifying media of the council, was due to Mr. Brando's power to secure ads from the local businessmen.

Exchanges and the Little League

The second and by far the most crucial way in which Du Pont handled its organizational dilemma was through the establishment of the Little League. In the Du Pont neighborhood in 1956 there was almost no communication between white and nonwhite working- and lower-class people, who together made up 90 percent of the neighborhood population. It was obvious that this communication barrier had to be bridged, and the Little League was organized with this objective in mind rather than for purely recreational purposes.

Money for equipment, coaches for the teams, umpires, players, and organizational know-how were the needed resources. Although Du Pont could have managed without the resources of the Catholic churches, the council did not wish to start a league made up only of the settlement house and the Protestant missions. A decision to ensure that this separation did not occur had a lasting effect on the council.

There were those who felt that the council should form the Little League by independently soliciting money, recruiting players, and organizing teams on the basis of racial balance. However, this scheme was overridden by the decision to ask local organizations to raise their own money and sponsor their own teams and not to press for integrated teams. This decision was made on two grounds: first, there was no indication that the council itself could recruit the needed resources. Many of the Italian boys were already playing in other leagues based outside the area. Secondly, Du Pont wanted to involve working-class adults, white and nonwhite. There was no point in having middle-class coaches, for it was the sons of the working class, through their fathers, that Du Pont sought to influence. In addition, Du Pont wanted to involve the Roman Catholic churches. Thus, influencing isolated working-class adults would be nothing compared with influencing working-class adults who were deeply enmeshed in neighborhood social groups, such as the Catholic churches and the local political clubs.

The success of Du Pont's policy through the years is indicated by the Italian representation on the sports committee. Seventeen of the thirty men who attended sports committee meetings during the 1963 season were working-class Italians. An analysis of the exchanges made at the sports committee and its activities illuminates the reasons for its success.

Exchanges with Individuals

To be a member of the sports committee, one had to be a coach of a team. Since a great many working-class men possess athletic skill, they were well represented on the committee. Coaching a team earned the men recognition from the children as well as from neighborhood adults who turned out to see the games. Coaches marched in the annual sports parade as well as hobnobbed with the local politicos at the awards ceremonies. Positions of esteem, such as marshal of the parade and coach of the all-star team, were available to any coach whom the others sought to reward, as shown in the following quotation from the sports committee field notes:

There was considerable discussion about who would throw out the first ball on opening day. It was finally agreed that the representative from [St. T.] who had been active for many years in the committee would get the honor. [Mr. K.,] the chairman of the committee, was initially thought to be the one to throw out the ball. He made a long speech in which he said he wasn't interested in glory, yet most of his actions would indicate otherwise. An All-Star game will be played after the parade against a team from another league. Suggestions were made as to who should coach Du Pont's team. Once again [Mr. K.] was considered but passed over. [Mr. C.] felt that [Mr. M.] should be the coach because of his great experience.[4]

There were considerable rewards available to coaches at the meetings. In the disputes over rules and regulations, they could indulge their fantasies of managing big-league teams. At the weekly meetings the winning coaches received the praise of their fellows when the previous week's scores and the standings of the teams were announced. In addition, games were rehashed and rewards were increased through the retelling of events. Rivalry between some men, which was close to the surface and easily noticeable at the meetings, heightened the rewards of attendance. The field notes state:

The rules and regulations in a way ape the rules and regulations of major league baseball and in a sense this formalization of sports is a way of identifying with the major leagues for the men. They can fantasy themselves in much the same position as the major league coaches, managers and owners of teams. . . . Over and over again they repeat that they are really preventing delinquency. Yet they do not realize that much of what they do is for themselves as when they purchase and institute such trappings which give them status . . . as a loud speaker to announce the games, elaborate uniforms for the teams, a commissioner for the league.[5]

The process that evolved at meetings over the years was reward-producing. Parliamentary procedure was observed largely in the breach. Much joking and sociability occurred, and the committee at their meetings illustrated the great value of adequate socialization. For example, no matter how heated the argument, every man was given his full say. Verbal whippings were given to any man who denied another this privilege. Praise was given to those who spoke eloquently.

It is conceivable that no matter how potentially rewarding a commit-tee's activities may be, unless it has developed a set of well-articulated norms to follow in achieving rewards, as did the Du Pont Sports Com-mittee, confusion and antagonisms concerning appropriate behavior will result. These may so raise the costs of participation that the potential rewards are nullified.

Exchanges with Organizations

Rewards were also available to individuals in their status of organi-zational representative, for a coach's activities with the ball team gave him added prestige in his home organization. There were also rewards to the organization. The rivalry between the two Catholic churches was an open secret, and a winning team meant added prestige to the organization. An argument that developed over which team would be first in line in the parade is indicative of this battle for prestige:

[Mr. M.] asked, "Why was I last last year?" He made a motion that this year his team be first. A vote was taken and his motion defeated. It was then decided to pull names out of a hat. [Saint J.,] which [Mr. M.] represents, pulled 7 out of 8. As the names were pooled [Mr. L.] and [Mr. K.] laughed harder and harder with each number. [Mr. M.] got extremely angry. He and [Mr. N.] of [Saint K.] began yelling at each other. [Saint J.] and [Saint K.] are in conflict in a number of areas. [Saint J.] is thought to have more pres-tigious members. [Mr. N.] finally said, "I was thrilled the way the numbers came out."[6]

The constant complaint of the sports committee was that it needed money. However, when one of the churches, Saint T., claimed to have an in with a large money-granting agency, representatives of Saint K. suddenly toned down the demand for money. On this occasion one of the coaches, referring to Saint K., said to the researcher, "They didn't want the other church to get the prestige."

Rivalries that existed among Negroes, Puerto Ricans, and Italians, as well as between Catholics and Protestants, were played out on the ball field as well as in the sports committee. Over the years there were con-stant allegations on the part of Negroes and Puerto Ricans that they were given raw deals in scheduling, protests, and decisions on the field. A coach had to attend sports committee meetings to defend his organization, his ethnic group, and his religion.

Winning the play-offs in the Little League was a sought-after reward, for the winning organization received a large trophy as well as medals for its players. Saint K. went so far as to have an award night to raise funds for its winning team. No mention at all was made of the fact that the Du Pont Council had supplied part of the awards.

The amount of money allocated for sports awards was a constant source of contention between the council's executive committee and the sports committee. Another source of tension was the insistence of the Roman Catholic churches that they not be involved in political activities. For example, the following transpired at a discussion about the sports parade:

[Mr. M.] of [Saint K.] spoke vehemently about not allowing politicians and even the chairman of the Council to make speeches at the first game after the parade. [Mr. T.] had previously spoken angrily about the chairman using the sports committee as a base for politics.[7]

The representatives from [Saint J.], [Mr. G.] and [Mr. M.], were quite upset about the parade. It seems that certain local politicians who were uninvited got into the lead car at the front of the parade, and gave the impression by their activities that the league was their affair. [Mr. M.] of [Saint K.] demanded that a letter of protest be sent.[8]

Concern seemed centered not so much on the politicians in general but on those politicians who were not supported by the Catholic churches. Clearly, then, the Catholic organizations did not want to provide rewards to politicians whom they did not favor.

Effects of the Exchanges

The Roman Catholic organizations were concerned lest the resources they hoped to exchange for Little League baseball be used for other purposes. Dahl is instructive about this possibility:

Although the kinds and amounts of resources available to political man are always limited and at any given moment fixed, they are not . . . permanently fixed as to either kind or amount. Political man can use his resources to gain influence, and he can then use his influence to gain more resources. Political resources can be pyramided in much the same way that a man who starts out in business sometimes pyramids a small investment into a large corporate empire.[9]

The Little League gave Du Pont an opportunity to pyramid its resources. These added resources created changes in the council as well as the neighborhood.

The neighborhood.   Voluntary organizations are a kind of "influence bank."[10] They not only are places where influence can be borrowed or procured, but they also increase the amount of influence available in a system. It was possible for Du Pont to develop considerable influence over local organizations by offering a major negotiable reward that these organizations sought, that is, prestige through the sports committee.

The sports committee meetings were the best attended and most lively that the council sponsored. Not only were individuals vying for influence over the group, but organizations were in direct conflict and competition for the available rewards. The two Catholic churches competed constantly. As noted, the Negro and Puerto Rican teams, which were largely Protestant, often complained that they had been given the short end of protests, scheduling disputes, and the like, by the other groups. The sports committee was an arena in which the various organizations, on the surface occupied only with sports, were actually contesting for prestige and symbols of power, which could be used as potent sources of influence in many of their own endeavors, such as recruiting members or raising money.

The sports committee was truly an influence bank, but the organizations had to pay a price for the influence they gained. This price included the loss of control over resources once they were invested, as well as the inability to stop investing the resources. For example, when some of the Catholic organizations on the sports committee, which were hostile to the council as an organization, sought to get the committee to secede from the council, it became apparent that the Protestant missions and the settlement house would not secede. The Catholic church that had sparked the secession movement then was forced to tone down its attacks on the council. Privately, one of the members of this church told the researcher, "If we would have pulled out ourselves, everyone would have said we broke up the League and we were prejudiced." In this case the council exerted great influence because secession meant a theatened loss of organizational prestige. The amount of influence available had been increased; five years earlier it would have been impossible for the Protestants to force the Catholics to do anything.

Even more unthinkable at the outset would have been the idea that concern over racial prejudice would have an effect on the organizational functioning of the non-Protestant organizations. Yet the establishment of the Little League did have a strong effect in this area. White, Negro, and Puerto Rican men came to know one another as well as to cooperate in a common cause. Up to this time the children had had little contact because Italian children by and large went to parochial school, and Negro and Puerto Rican children attended public school. Now children of all races, instead of being complete strangers, got to know one another. More importantly, adults got to know these children. Some informants felt that this last accomplishment was perhaps the most crucial factor in lessening violence in the neighborhood.

Although over the years there were minor squabbles during games and a few near riots, ultimately a norm that coaches had to control their players was developed. A coach who failed to do so was openly censured at committee meetings. Sports was perhaps the one area that could unite the groups in Du Pont. Families often came to watch their children play; often hundreds of people watched a game. The Little League became the symbol of the Du Pont Council's main principle— that racial integration was possible and desirable. Many of those who invested their resources in the Little League and actually did the most to make integration come true initially, at least, would never have agreed with the principle.

The council. Looking at the rewards available through the sports committee, one can discern long-term and short-term rewards of considerable variety that were available to organizations and to individuals in their various status positions. The success of the sports committee in creating rewards is especially interesting in the light of what is known about lower-working-class participation in community affairs. The committee, through its structure and procedures, offered to the working-class man rewards of respect and deference and also rewards related to the exercise of power and the occupation of honorific positions.[11] Significantly, very few of them ever became active in the affairs of the council. In general, they simply did not possess the requisites needed to participate in other council committees.

Cohen and Hodges point out that even if a working-class man values the goals of the organization and believes in giving it generalized support, he does not feel that his influence within the organization is such that his active participation would make an important difference in how things turn out. Certain attitudes of the more unstable working class also deter participation in a council: a preference for the familiar, a distaste for slow and methodical planning, a bent toward authoritarian patterns of decision-making, intolerance of minority groups, and a pervasive fatalism.[12] These attitudes raise the costs of participation.

The segregation of working-class men into a single committee where they could maximize their rewards and lower their costs was a device that enabled them to function in the council, albeit not without strain and conflict. Instead of allowing the council to become only a debating society for the white, liberal, middle-class professionals, unable to influence anyone but themselves, the Little League gave the council a means of communicating with working-class groups and bridging the conflict of interest with the Italian organizations. It also gave the council a great source of stability. Year in and year out the Little League went on, and individuals, groups, and organizations invested their resources. Other programs came and went. Some succeeded, some failed, but none had the kind of impact on the neighborhood or the council that the Little League had. For most people in the neighborhood the council was synonymous with the Little League.

Summary

It should not be assumed from this chapter that Du Pont became a paradise of racial amity. However, significant changes occurred in the community as a result of the organization of the council. Essentially, prior to 1956, if one had resources that he wanted to use to influence the neighborhood's racial attitudes, there was no place to exchange them for this type of influence. In the area of race relations in Du Pont in 1956, there was, in effect, an informal system of influence in which no one assumed responsibility for the influence he exerted. What Du Pont attempted to do was to control the community by making local organizations assume responsibility for race relations through a more formal system.[13]

Although there were few resources available in the Italian-oriented organizations for bettering race relations, there were substantial amounts available for baseball. These resources, once committed, afforded the council an opportunity to use them in ways other than strictly for baseball. Through this means, as well as through recruiting highly respected Italians as chairman, Du Pont solved a major problem, the recruitment of the resources necessary to achieve its main organizational end. In the 1963 sports parade the lead banner, carried by a white and a Negro Little Leaguer, read, "Side by Side for a Better East Side." It symbolized the prestige and vitality of the council and, as such, enhanced the council's ability to enter into exchanges.

NOTES

1. Alvin W. Gouldner, "The Secrets of Organizations," *The Social Welfare Forum*, Proceedings of the National Conference on Social Welfare, Cleveland, 1963 (New York: Columbia University Press, 1963), p. 171.

2. William H. Form, "Stratification in Low and Middle Income Housing Areas," *Journal of Social Issues*, VII, nos. 1, 2 (1951), 120.

3. In his study of councils in England, N. Dennis observed that those which survived were able to replace their leadership when it was no longer adequate to the tasks required of it. See N. Dennis, "Change in Function and Leadership Renewal: A Case Study of the Community Association Movement and Problems of Voluntary Small Groups in the Urban Locality," *Sociological Research*, IX (March 1961), 59.

4. Du Pont Sports Committee field notes, May 8, 1963. Such notes were kept for each of the Du Pont meetings and activities that the research team attended. The outline used in recording field observations is reproduced in Appendix C, "Outline for Field Observations."

5. Ibid., April 2, 1963.

6. Ibid., May 8, 1963.

7. Ibid., March 20, 1963.

8. Ibid., May 14, 1963.

9. Robert A. Dahl, *Who Governs: Democracy and Power in an American City* (New Haven: Yale University Press, 1961), p. 226.

10. Talcott Parsons, "On the Concept of Influence," *Public Opinion Quarterly*, XXVII (Spring 1963), 61.

11. "The satisfactions that derive from participation itself consist largely of respect and deference, which in turn are linked to the exercise of power, the occupation of honorific positions, and the quality of performance of one's organizational roles. These latter, in turn, rest upon the possession of relevant skills and personal qualities: knowledge about the goals of the organization and the aspects of the larger social scene that are relevant to the attainment of these goals; fluency in discussion and argumentation; special combinations of discipline, restraint, initiative and sensitivity that are necessary to perform successfully in committee operations; certain technical skills; parliamentary, clerical, bookkeeping, fiscal. These are the same kind of skills and personal qualities that the lower working class, in comparison to other strata, has the least opportunity to acquire, cultivate and practice in the world of work and the universalistic achievement sector" (Albert K. Cohen and Harold M. Hodges, Jr., "Characteristics of the Lower-Blue-Collar Class," *Social Problems*, X [Spring 1963], 315–16).

12. Ibid., pp. 316–25.

13. Formal and informal systems of influence are discussed by James Coleman, "Comment on the Concept of Influence," *Public Opinion Quarterly*, XXVII (Spring 1963), 70. Informal influence refers to the type of influence movie stars, for example, have over teen-agers, where there is no accountability. Formal influence refers to the type of influence teachers have over teen-agers, where there are certain controls on how the influence is exerted.

5

The Newspaper
and Education

IN DU PONT, as probably in all councils, there was never a shortage of projects. The problem always revolved around finding the resources to carry out the projects. Councils generally solve this problem in one of three ways: by recruiting the resources and doing the project themselves; by coordinating the activities of other organizations that possess the needed resources, as Du Pont did with the Little League; or by persuading other organizations to carry out the project.

This last method is perhaps the most difficult to achieve and the one most often attempted. What is more sensible than to go to the park commissioner and state the case for a needed new park, or to the board of education for a new school, or to the police commissioner for more police. Although it is obvious to a neighborhood group that it needs a new school, it is usually not obvious until the group goes to the Board of Education that there are insufficient resources available to build all the new schools needed. Thus to get the school, at the least the group must be prepared for a long struggle. It took Du Pont five years to get a replacement for PS 4.

Once the first burst of enthusiasm wears off—after four or five delegations have plodded to the board of education, the city planning commission, and the city council without concrete results—a council faces another organizational dilemma. This problem is equal in severity to that caused by conflicts of interest in the neighborhood. The dilemma

53

is twofold: (1) how to muster the influence to achieve the goal, and (2) how to maintain the council as a viable organization during the time it will take to achieve the goal.

Exchanges and the Du Pont News

The success in school controversies of influence techniques, such as boycotts, sit-ins, and freedom schools, can be related to the political climate engendered by the civil rights movement as well as the national implications of racial segregation in the schools. The problem of a replacement for PS 4 had no civil rights significance, and segregation was never an issue. Thus the council was left to its own devices to develop the needed influence and remain alive as an organization.

A major asset that the council had at its disposal was the *Du Pont News*. The style and format was professional and probably would have won an award had there been competition for neighborhood papers. It was published four or five times a year, generally at periods when advertisements could most easily be procured—election time, Christmas, graduation, Easter. When something special was in the offing, an extra issue was usually published. A local Boy Scout troop distributed it free to most neighborhood families. The paper was vital to the council's existence.

The newspaper committee met ten times during 1962–1963, with an average attendance of eight. There were fifteen members in all. The rewards to individuals were varied. An amateur photographer served as the staff photographer; one man wrote a historical column, another editorials, etc. There were many rewards for job accomplishment and meetings were pleasant. Two women counted words in articles and reread articles. When they finished, they generally made coffee and served cake, which one of them had baked. Others collected money for ads, and one man simply cut out old advertisements that were to be used again.

The editor not only was gifted in editorial skills, but was also a master at making participation on the newspaper as rewarding as possible. Instead of merely writing the editorials, he read them aloud at meetings and invited comment. When policies were set, everyone was given a chance to have his say. All these activities occurred informally. One informant felt that the newspaper committee was really similar to the executive committee, since all the important matters in the council and the neighborhood were discussed at these meetings. Without question, members of the newspaper committee were more committed to the council than members of any other committee, with the exception of the executive. On a personal level, emotional, service, ideological, and negotiable rewards were available to participants.

Effect on Council and Neighborhood

The paper gave the council a way of communicating with the neighborhood and, in fact, was the one real, clear symbol of the council to the neighborhood. The editor often was able to use the newspaper to promote policies that the council favored. In addition, the paper provided rewards to local organizations. Businesses had a cheap source of advertisements. Local politicos watched the pages of the *Du Pont News* closely lest a rival gain free publicity. Churches all announced their events. The newspaper was a useful mechanism of exchange for the council.

Although some members viewed their participation on the paper as a pleasant hobby and were willing to invest the evenings of work on that basis alone, others, especially the editor, knew that the *Du Pont News* was a powerful resource for the council. Having no other competition in the neighborhood, it could at least give currency to the council's point of view. Without doubt, the *News* gave the council the image of being a substantial organization, not only in the neighborhood but also in the larger community. It was always mailed to city officials whom the council wished to impress, praise, or criticize.

In the long battle over replacing PS 4, the paper not only kept the issue alive in the neighborhood, but it kept it alive for city officials, as articles from three issues of different years prove:

The Du Pont area was represented at the Board of Estimate hearing on the capital budget for school construction at City Hall on November 17. . . . The urgent needs of our area, outlined in detail by Du Pont representatives . . . brought to the Board's attention that these schools are all obsolete and dilapidated, having outlived their usefulness as school buildings.[1]

Representatives of the Du Pont neighborhood joined others in protesting before the City Planning Commission the sharp reductions in much-needed school construction which had been proposed for the 1961 Capital Budget.[2]

BOARD OF EDUCATION NIXES SMITH SITE FOR P. S. 4 [headline atop page 1]. Turned down on its attempts to have P. S. 4 . . . placed on Tanahey Park, the Du Pont community was stunned by another setback when Adrian Bloomenfeld, administrator of school planning and research for the Board of Education, rejected local citizens' proposal that the new school be built on the site of the present Cherry St. Gym at Cherry and Catherine Streets.[3]

While seeking to unite the neighborhood against outside school officials, at the same time the council fostered through the *Du Pont News* a policy of cooperation with neighborhood school administrators. Large pictures and favorable stories about the principals and superintendents in the area were often featured. An editorial in a 1958 issue clearly illustrated this policy:

PATIENCE AND FORTITUDE [headline]. It is particularly good advice for the parents of this community whose children will be going to double and triple sessions. . . . Idle worry and nervous rumor spreading will not hasten the construction of the new school by one day. It will only make life more difficult for other parents, for the pupils themselves, and for the teachers and school administrators who will be doing their best in a difficult situation.[4]

This kind of editorial helped to gain the council an important resource—access to the local schools and their officials who possessed vital information that the council needed to make effective presentations at public and private hearings with outside officials. Though not the only mechanism that the council used to set up an exchange of resources with the local school officialdom, the newspaper was extremely useful to the other instruments of exchange, particularly the education committee.

Exchanges and the Education Committee

Concern of parents over the reading levels of their children helped lead to the formation of the Du Pont Council. The realization that a group of citizens could bring about changes in the schools, such as the remedial-reading program instituted in Du Pont, gave impetus to the drive to get a replacement for PS 4 and also to the formation of the education committee.

The call for this committee was sounded in a *Du Pont News* editorial in April 1957 entitled "Let's Get Together." It read:

Here is our suggestion. Let the officers of the Parents' Associations of our neighborhood schools—Junior High School 65, Public Schools 1, 29, and 4, and St. John and St. Christopher Parochial Schools—get together to decide what are our biggest school problems. Then with the help of the Education Division of HEED, they can start finding out what it will take to do something about schools for our children.[5]

Almost six years to the day elapsed between the call for this committee and the appropriation of money for the replacement of PS 4. During this interim the education committee was able to muster the resources necessary to achieve this goal as well as many others. The exchanges it effected illuminate considerably the reasons for its success.

Exchanges with Organizations

The call for all the parents' associations to unite was responded to only by the public-school parents' associations. The education committee thus faced the same problem as did the council in general—how to involve the Roman Catholic organizations. In addition, it faced the difficult job of maintaining the cooperation of the public-school parents' associations, when these organizations had their own problems. Women with young children have limited time to give to organizational life.

One way in which cooperation was secured was by sponsoring programs that strengthened the local parents' associations. These programs also had the effect of strengthening the education committee. Each year from 1959 to 1963, the Du Pont education committee sponsored a Brotherhood Week celebration in February and a UNICEF carnival in October that attracted five hundred to one thousand children and adults. These two events provided the parents' associations with two successful annual programs and relieved them of the pressure of having to plan a program for each of their monthly meetings. These programs were also great morale boosters, which countered some of their poorly attended meetings and programs.

The council certainly drew prestige from these educational programs. The education committee also was provided with a source of rewards that supplied stability during the years of frustration from sending delegation after delegation to city officials in its school replacement efforts.

The carnival and the Brotherhood Week celebrations also enabled the council to involve the Catholic parents' associations in the education committee. One key informant felt that the prime reason for mounting these programs was to involve the Catholic parents' associations. Replacing PS 4 was not of much concern to them, for they had replacement problems in their own parochial schools.

Exchanges with Individuals

It must be remembered that it was the individual members of the parents' association who had to invest their time and effort, and who personally experienced the frustrations and delay. Although in their roles as parents' association chairmen and officers there were rewards—from programs that the education committee enabled them to sponsor—this fact alone probably does not account for the resources these

individuals invested in the education committee. The following letter
to the editor of the *Du Pont News* gives some indication of the costs
involved in participation:

Dear Editor: Jr. H. S. 65 was scheduled to speak at the Board of Estimate
Hearing on the Education Expense Budget at City Hall on April 15th. I
had sent in my request to speak at a very early date, and I had been told
that there were not too many requests in at that time. . . . Your turn to speak
is based on when you submit your request. I spent six hours at the hearing
waiting to be called, and then I had alternates there until 7:30 PM and our
school had not been called during all that time. . . . Something should be
done about this situation.[6]

This experience was certainly not rewarding but typified the committee's difficulties. The parents' association chairmen brought with
them great experience and know-how about the rules, regulations, and
procedures of the board of education and other city departments. To
overcome the frustrations and to retain such individuals who possessed
the needed resources, the council capitalized on negotiable rewards
that it could offer, such as making it possible to climb a civic opportunity ladder. The chairman of the education committee in 1962 went
on to be the HEED cochairman of education, then on to activity in
citywide parents' associations, and ultimately into politics. Opportunities such as these are potent sources of influence on those members of
a community who seek such organizational affiliations.[7]

The council's getting money replaced on the city's 1963 capital budget for PS 4, in the words of seasoned political observers, was "unheard
of." Due to council members' knowledge of the political system, they
discovered that they could not get a new school because the housing
department, the parks department and the board of education had
been unable to come to an agreement over a site and had, therefore,
postponed the building of the school. It was an established practice for
these departments to trade land to one another, as well as to perform
other favors, but in the case of PS 4 one or more of them decided to
hold out for a better bargaining position. The chairman of the education committee happened to be an effective public speaker, and at a
board of estimate hearing, she pointed out that Du Pont was being
denied a school because three departments were not talking to one
another. At this point the mayor insisted that the three get together.
Money was reappropriated and construction was begun in 1964.

This particular problem could not have been solved without real
knowledge of the political process, as well as the rules, regulations, and

procedures of the board of education. The survival of the committee and this major success can be related to the committee's ability to offer rewards to organizations in their various interrelationships, that is, the parents' associations and the council, and to individuals in their various statuses, that is, parents and clubwomen who had the resources needed in this situation.

Effects of the Exchanges

The replacement of PS 4 was not the only victory of the education committee. It pressed for and succeeded in getting after-school recreational programs in the local schools and a new cafeteria for Junior High 65. It moved the board of education to consider that the dominant emphasis in textbooks and schools on middle-class, white standards and individuals might have adverse effects on Negroes and Puerto Ricans.

Mrs. Lipkoff proposed a program to bring into one of the local schools a sense of respect for the work of men of all races and cultures. It was so well received by all who heard that a "Hall of Heroes" has been inaugurated in P. S. 4 with pictures and captions of people of many cultures. . . . Through the Du Pont Education Committee, HEED incorporated these thoughts into its report at the Board of Estimate hearing. The hearing was at once electrified—questions, statements, answers filled the room. The Board of Education has, as a result of the hearing, moved more quickly to bring a deeper study of the humanities into the lives of our children.[8]

This interest was aroused several years before such activities became more prevalent.

When the education committee began in 1957, it did not possess either the knowledge or the influence to achieve its goals. However, over a period of time it was possible for the committee to exchange the rewards it produced for the required resources. Although it could be argued that from the point of view of school needs, a Brotherhood Week celebration was unimportant, the annual program brought all the parents' associations together under the aegis of the council and served to establish a coalition of these organizations. Thus under the council's education committee the parents' associations became a potent force in relation to education in the neighborhood. The Du Pont committee's natural connection with HEED's education committee and its link to the local school board through the board's chairman, Reverend Older, helped to form a larger coalition for improving education in the neighborhood—one that was hard to defeat.

Often parents' associations are controlled by principals who select the chairmen and plan the programs. By forming a coalition of parents' associations, Du Pont to an extent took control of the parents' associations from the principals. Committee meetings were not held in schools. The ramifications of issues in one school were related to other schools, and points of view on various problems were broadened. It was more often the council that defined a school problem than a school principal.

In a few years the council had made a deep impact on the neighborhood. Prior to its existence, school affairs had been largely in the hands of school professionals. Though in the main the professionals still controlled the schools, Du Pont had become a group whose ideas had to be considered. The local superintendent acted in peremptory fashion toward community groups; however, by 1963 the best she could do was compromise with the council. When Du Pont wanted to set up a remedial-reading program for after-school hours, she was angered at not being kept abreast of all developments. Had the time been the middle 1950s, the project would probably never have been completed, given her reputation of willfulness. In 1963 she was able only to stall the project for a few weeks and cause a change in name to homework-helper program.

This emerging influence of Du Pont in education was not lost on others who sought to influence the school system. One of the local school principals was a man with many innovative ideas about education. In the somewhat rigid hierarchy of the school system, the willful local superintendent posed a huge stumbling block for him. Du Pont offered this principal an opportunity to pyramid his own resources. The first meeting to plan the remedial-reading program was held in his office.

The success of any one committee in the council cannot be divorced from the successes or failures of other committees. The newspaper helped the education committee, which helped the housing committee. Through the education committee's constant appearances at City Hall over the years, it made city officials aware that a Du Pont neighborhood existed and that the council was not another of those fly-by-night citizens' groups that die as fast as they are born. When in 1960 the housing committee began its push for an urban-renewal plan, the city planning commission was already aware of the activities of Du Pont. Prestige was useful to the council in arranging exchanges.

Summary

Most of the recent sociological writing about organizations is based on the hypothesis that an organization must perform self-maintenance functions (internal integration and external stabilization) and goal-attainment functions (achievement of goals and procurement of the resources necessary for goal achievement).[9] An overemphasis on either set of functions could potentially destroy an organization. The immediate danger that beginning councils in their desire to control neighborhood conditions would seem to face, then, is their overcommitment to goal attainment.

Most dangerous is an overcommitment to such goals as getting a new park, a new school, or better housing. The dilemma that a council sometimes faces is how to maintain itself if a long time period is required to muster the resources to achieve these goals. Du Pont's experience with PS 4 demonstrates how survival for long periods of time is crucial for council goal attainment. By organizing the UNICEF carnivals and the Brotherhood Week celebrations, the education committee was able to achieve its goal of a replacement for PS 4 by offering short-term exchanges to sustain the participants until the long-term payoff.

The ability of the Du Pont Education Committee to offer rewards to participants in statuses other than that of organizational representative is certainly one other crucial factor that accounts for its success in coordinating the efforts of the local parents' associations and the failure of other such committees in coordinating other organizations in joint ventures.[10] By hooking itself into an opportunity ladder in the educational system, the council preserved for the committee those members who had vital resources of knowledge and expertise.[11] In political battles over school replacement, the ability to persevere is often of crucial importance. Du Pont's ability to do this was clearly enhanced by its reward structure.

NOTES

1. *Du Pont News*, December 18, 1959, p. 3.
2. Ibid., November 4, 1960, p. 1.
3. Ibid., November 2, 1962, p. 1.
4. Ibid., June 13, 1958, p. 2.
5. Ibid., April 5, 1957, p. 2.
6. Ibid., May 2, 1958, p. 2.
7. It should be remembered that the people who consciously seek the negotiable rewards that councils offer might also manipulate a council away from its avowed ends toward their own purposes. Thus their participation might be either functional or dysfunctional for council survival and goal attainment.
8. *Du Pont News*, February 11, 1960, p. 1.

9. Talcott Parsons, "Suggestions for a Sociological Approach to the Theory of Organizations," *Complex Organizations,* ed. Amitai Etzioni (New York: Holt, Rinehart and Winston, 1961), pp. 42–47.

10. Status-set refers to the number of statuses an individual occupies. For a discussion of this concept and its relation to role-set, see Robert K. Merton, *Social Theory and Social Structure* (Glencoe, Ill.: Free Press, 1957), pp. 368–84.

11. It is not suggested that the rewards of climbing the opportunity ladder were the only things that kept the members active. Certainly the belief that a new school was needed played a part in their activity.

6

Politics and Government

Skill in politics is defined by Dahl as the ability to gain more influence than others using the same resources.[1] By this definition, the Du Pont Council possessed some master politicians. Not only were they able to gain influence over certain specific governmental decisions, such as when a new school was to be built, but, as will be described in this chapter, they were able to a degree to effect significant changes in the total neighborhood political system. Dahl further notes:

Most of the time . . . most citizens use their resources for purposes other than gaining influence over government decisions. There is a great gap between their actual influence and their potential influence. Their political resources are, so to speak, *slack* [emphasis added] in the system. In some circumstances these resources might be converted from nonpolitical purposes.[2]

The conversion of slack resources into influence over governmental decisions is a major task of neighborhood councils. The genesis of most councils lies in the realization that voting once a year can have little influence over whether a neighborhood gets more police protection, better recreational facilities, and the like. The hope is always that a council can gain the needed influence. Yet converting slack resources is a difficult procedure. The resources may be slack for any number of reasons: commitment to other demands, such as those by family, church, or friends; attitudes and values that preclude commitment to

63

political objectives; fear of the costs involved in committing the resources, etc. Thus great insight is required to understand just where the slack resources are in a neighborhood and how to utilize them to achieve desired ends.

To understand why councils have difficulty recruiting slack resources, one further aspect must be considered: the actual opposition of local organizations. If a council should succeed in gaining influence over governmental agencies in regard to the services these agencies supply the neighborhood, what is the function of the local political club or a councilman's office or a more informal power structure? The greatest cost one organization can impose upon another is to take over one of its vital reward-producing functions. At the least, a successful council implies that a local political leader is not all-powerful and that there are alternate ways of getting things done. At the most, a successful council must appear to a politician in a political club as a potential rival club that might contend for local leadership.

Thus, a council must be prepared to deal with opposition, covert and overt, from organizations to which it poses a threat. Most often, opposing organizations are older and have greater resources with which to oppose a new council, as was certainly the case in the Du Pont Council's relationship to politics in its neighborhood. Yet after eight years the council was not only surviving, but it had considerably altered the local political picture.

Exchanges and Politics

Since the late 1920s Du Pont had in most elections returned five- or six-to-one majorities for the Democrats. A national Democratic candidate had been born within its boundaries, and the local Democratic club was the most influential organization in the neighborhood. Each Thursday night its doors were open to those who needed work, intercession with the police, help with immigration problems or a landlord, etc. The most influential man in the neighborhood was the leader of the Democratic club, a man known as the Count. Until the council became active in the late 1950s, the Count's hegemony over his domain had virtually been complete. His only competition was a small Republican club that was made up of a few dissidents and whose existence was made possible by the patronage of the Republican-controlled state legislature. By 1962 the Count's position was no longer so secure.

Until the early 1960s both the Democratic and the Republican clubs were dominated by Italians and Jews. The usual pattern was to have an Italian leader and a Jewish co-leader. In the 1950s because Negro and Puerto Rican votes were not critical to political success, the Republicans did not seriously court them and the Count did not need them. It was, therefore, natural that Negro and Puerto Rican representation was minimal at the Thursday night clubhouse "help" sessions. By 1963 this situation had changed drastically, with both parties actively recruiting the increasingly important Negro and Puerto Rican voter.

Exchanges with Organizations

When the council came into existence, it offered considerable rewards to the local political groups. People were in a state of panic because of gang warfare, vandalism, and strained race relations. However, these problems were foreign to the usual Thursday night open house at the club. The clubhouse's approach to social problems had been on a one-by-one basis. The availability of a nonpartisan group that emphasized recreation and public safety and was willing to take on these social problems was probably viewed initially not as a threat to the political clubs, but as a help in maintaining the status quo. In addition, when Mr. Brando was elected council chairman in early 1957, the Count no doubt allayed any fears that he might have had, since he and Brando had been close friends since boyhood.

The Count did not actively oppose Du Pont but actually helped when asked, as the following lead article in the *Du Pont News* illustrates (Assemblyman Salvatio was a member of the Democratic club and was known as one who carried out the Count's wishes):

It snowed, it rained, it hailed; but like the traditional mailman neither snow nor rain nor hail could keep Harry Salvatio, Charles Perry, Isidore Bloom . . . from their appointment with Richard C. Jenkins, . . . supervisor, Department of Parks, to discuss proposals of the Du Pont Neighborhood Council for improving Colencan Oval. . . . Credit for assistance in gaining four of the community's seven points goes to Assemblyman Salvatio and Mr. Perry as well as Mike Palumbo, who drew up blueprints that were used in the presentation.[3]

It can be assumed that such free publicity in the *Du Pont News* was a reward not overlooked by Assemblyman Salvatio or the Count. With Brando as council chairman from 1957 to 1959 and several of the Count's political associates active in the sports committee, if the Count gave Du Pont any thought at all, he must have seen it as an organization that he could influence more than it could influence him.

The situation began to change in 1959. An article in the *Du Pont*

News the year before about a rent hike in the middle-income project was a harbinger of this change:

> T.V. tenants received a big jolt in their family budgets this week when new rents . . . went into effect. . . . An ironic aftermath of the rent fight was the struggle by the two local political clubs to grab for the glory of having fought the increase on behalf of the tenants. John T. Mussela, leader of the Lower East End Republican Club, and J. J. Pagano, leader of the A.E.S. Democratic Club, traded news releases and open letters to the tenants patting themselves on the back for having presented the tenants' case at the hearings.[4]

The Du Pont Council had suddenly set itself up as the judge of the politicians. At this point, the council must have appeared as a mixed blessing to the Count and his Republican opponents.

In the summer of 1959 gang warfare and neighborhood reaction to it reached a high point, as was recorded by the Du Pont staff worker at the time:

> On Sunday night there was an eruption of teen violence in HEED which saw a number of fights and the death of a teenage girl on Avenue D. Another boy died later that night. . . . The community woke up with a hangover on Monday morning. Although nothing occurred in our Du Pont area, there was a feeling of nausea and despair.[5]

Du Pont's response to this situation was to organize a Town Hall meeting to give people an opportunity to air their feelings and to stimulate interest in the council's programs. Between four-hundred and five-hundred people turned out. This meeting signaled a change in the relationship between the council and neighborhood political groups. Note the following record:

> The political repercussions have been more significant than we judged during the planning phase. One criticism often heard was that it was a Republican meeting since Mr. Mussela was moderator. . . . I have also heard that . . . the Democratic club representative during the planning stage was "on the carpet" for allowing a Republican to be so heavily featured. However, . . . the female Democratic district co-leader did sit on the panel platform even though she was not invited to do so. Finally, State Senator Borro, who came late to the meeting, was not asked to sit on the platform, and there were reactions to this.[6]

After the Town Hall meeting it was clear that Du Pont could offer rewards to politicians for participation and that there were obvious costs for nonparticipation. As an aftermath of this meeting, politicians watched one another lest one gain some advantage through his activities in the council. In fact, around election times, whenever a politician was mentioned in the *Du Pont News* gossip column, no matter how casually, the others almost always bitterly complained.

The council's ability to enter into exchanges with the local politicians was also enhanced when the sports committee decided to sponsor a parade in the spring of 1959, to raise money for the Little League. The committee asked the local political leaders, among others, to attend. Thousands of people witnessed this parade. Every tenement window had someone in it, since this was the first parade the Du Pont neighborhood had ever had. The opportunity to appear surrounded by happy children before potential voters was not lost on the politicians. As noted in a previous chapter, an unexpected feature of the 1963 parade was the uninvited appearance of several political aspirants in the lead automobile.

The sudden emergence in 1959 of the Du Pont Council as a force in the neighborhood was not something that the Count relished:

George [L.] said that this [the Republican prominence at the Town Hall Meeting] is also why the Democratic club has thus far failed to send its annual $200 contribution for the Du Pont Little League program.[7]

This threatened withdrawal of funds did not materialize, perhaps because the Count, with his five-to-one majority over the Republicans, was not really frightened or perhaps because he felt that a threat was all that was needed to make the council realize its interest lay in cooperating with him.

Had the council done nothing else, no doubt the Count could have limited its political influence. However, by 1959 Rev. Mr. Older and several of the other leaders of Du Pont's coalition had agreed that the Negroes and Puerto Ricans had to be given political power if they were to be truly integrated in the neighborhood. They felt that the local political clubs—the centers of reward allocation—had to be made more responsive to Negro and Puerto Rican needs. The coalition also realized that the council must not alienate either of the regular clubs, since these groups provided the council with such resources as money for sports, contacts at City Hall, etc. The charge of political partisanship by either one of the groups could severely weaken the council. Sensitivity to the council's need of resources for survival and goal attainment helped the coalition to make its decision to foster, informally and outside the council, the formation of insurgent Democratic and Republican clubs. Thus in 1960 and 1961 a reform Democratic club and an insurgent Republican club were started. These new clubs immensely strengthened the council's ability to make exchanges with the local politicians. No longer could the Count and his associates take their positions for granted.

In explaining this tactic, Rev. Mr. Older said, "The crucial task of a neighborhood council is not to solve every problem but to know how and where every problem can best be solved." He reasoned that the Du Pont neighborhood was so overwhelmingly Democratic that even a swing of all Negro and Puerto Rican voters to the Republicans would not effectively challenge the Democrats. Negro and Puerto Rican votes might be crucial, however, in intraparty fights over leadership. This reasoning proved essentially correct. Although in the elections for district leadership in 1963 neither the Count nor his Republican counterpart was unseated, important changes did take place. Both regular groups were forced to offer Negroes and Puerto Ricans patronage jobs, as well as positions of some prestige in the respective clubs. As one Negro informant said, "We got our chance because the white men got into a fight."

These intraparty leadership fights gave the council a real resource to exchange—the possible use of the council by politicians to gain political advantage. Thus the Count was often forced to go along with the council's projects that formerly he had never been concerned with.

Exchanges with Individuals

Earlier it was indicated that a major organizational problem for a council is to persuade individuals to invest their slack resources in achieving the council's goals. Part of Du Pont's skill in this type of persuasion lay in the fact that it did not, in many cases, try to attract resources for the specific ends it wanted to achieve. The Du Pont Council never said, "Invest your resources with us so that we can change the corrupt political system." Had the council used this technique, it never would have gotten Mr. Brando to serve as council chairman or business manager of the *Du Pont News*, since he was the Count's personal friend. Yet without Brando, the *News*, a vital political resource for the council, would probably never have been put on a solvent basis. Thus Brando unwittingly did as much as any man in the neighborhood to weaken the Count's position. Other participants on the newspaper committee who saw the paper as a hobby or a source of sociability, as well as the members of the sports committee who invested their resources in a sports parade, also strengthened the council vis-à-vis the Count.

There were, of course, some slack resources that the council recruited in exchange for political rewards. The chairman of the council from 1959 to 1961 subsequently ran for state senator. The chairman from 1961 to 1963 revealed that he had first become interested in the council when he heard of and attended the Town Hall meeting on delinquency. He readily admitted that part of his initial motivation in joining the council was to make himself known to, as well as get to know, the Negro and Puerto Rican groups in the neighborhood. The council also provided one of the captains of the regular Democratic club opportunities to enhance his prestige with the Count. According to other members of the executive committee, his job was to keep the Count apprised of what the council was doing, as well as to present to the council the Count's point of view.

Effects of the Exchanges

Had the political groups been able to oppose the council, the council would have lost a major source of its influence in negotiations with city departments—namely, its claim to be a grass-roots organization representing the total neighborhood. This united front was important, for city departments are usually wary of becoming embroiled in local battles. At the least, local conflict can stall a project such as a new school or a housing development.

The Council. The city's acceptance of the Du Pont Self-Renewal Plan in 1961 was an example of how the council presented a united neighborhood point of view to city agencies. The plan provided for the construction of both middle- and low-income housing on land near a river where new buildings could be built without knocking down old ones and dispossessing tenants. Although there was no real basis for conflict within the neighborhood, meetings were held to acquaint various groups with the plan. A citywide planners' association gave the council an award for its originality, and the *Du Pont News* published maps and pictures, as well as articles like the following:

A dramatic development in the rebuilding of the Du Pont area occurred with the announcement by the City Planning Commission on May 1 that a substantial section of our community fronting the East River has been selected for a proposed Urban Renewal study under the Title I program. . . . The Self-Renewal program quickly won broad support in our community from numerous institutions, churches, agencies, elected representatives and officials of both parties.[8]

The political climate in the neighborhood, which the council had helped to create, made this united front possible.

When a few months later the city planning commission officially designated a Du Pont urban renewal area, the council had gained a major victory. Prior to the formation of the council, the neighborhood did not even have a name; Du Pont was the name that had been selected by members of the council.

Formulating an imaginative yet sound self-renewal plan required people with considerable technical competence. Du Pont was able to recruit people with the needed resources for a variety of reasons. Those with political skill sought and often gained the substantial rewards that the council offered to the politically inclined. For example, Mr. Point, who was chairman of the council when the award for the self-renewal plan was presented, shortly thereafter received the Republican nomination for state senator. Technical experts in housing and planning volunteered their services to the council, partly because they saw an opportunity to influence the city planning commission toward a favored building design. Since they were interested in pyramiding their resources, just as was the council, a mutually advantageous exchange took place.

Timely information is also an important resource.[9] Du Pont was able to recruit it. A Mr. Freeman, who was a member of a professional planners' association and was assisting Du Pont as a private citizen, was actually employed by the city planning commission as a staff planner. The privileged information that he passed on to the chairman of the council's housing committee was often crucial in the council's negotiations with the city.

The neighborhood. In the literature of community organization one of the major goals set forth for neighborhood councils is that they should act as one of the communication links between neighborhood and city.[10] The Du Pont Council was able to achieve this goal because the local political clubs were not functioning in the area of schools, parks, housing, and the like. The council's office walls were always lined with letters from city officials. Communications with the city were often deliberately handled in such a way as to allow city officials to confuse Du Pont with HEED, a much larger organization with considerable political influence. In addition, since several Du Pont members had informal ties with city officials in various departments, mutually advantageous exchanges of information were able to take place. Through the *Du Pont News* the council often was able to create interest in such matters as housing and schools.

All these factors had the effect of waking the city administration to the fact that there actually was a Du Pont neighborhood that needed its attention. A close observer of the neighborhood noted that because of the council's activities local politicians were beginning to make their influence felt at City Hall. The Count suddenly began talking about schools, housing, etc. Although the reform Democratic club had a part in stimulating the older club, the council clearly played a major part in activating what was at best a dormant communication link.

Perhaps the most subtle source of Du Pont's influence on the neighborhood lay in its existence for a period of years during which no other group viewed the whole neighborhood as its province nor attempted to define the rewards and costs related to civil rights, a new hospital, urban renewal, a new ball field, etc. A statement by Reitzes deserves quotation in this light:

Organizational structuring is effective to the extent that it defines the situation for the individual in terms of his special interests in the situation. . . . The Club [council] was effective because it provided the individual with well-formulated statements, reasons and justifications for his specific acts in specific situations. . . . It told him how to act, provided a structure and a set of procedures to reach the goal.[11]

Thus the Du Pont Council was able to develop influence not only by the way it defined a particular problem but also by virtue of the fact that it was the only voice on neighborhood problems to be heard clearly and consistently.

Due to its broad scope, the council was in time able to pyramid its resources. Few in 1956 would have thought that there was much hope for change in the political structure of the neighborhood. Yet in the fall of 1963 the council sponsored a successful voter-registration drive among Negro and Puerto Rican residents. This project was watched with some distrust by the regular clubs, but with the primary fights in the offing they could do nothing but cooperate lest votes go to the other groups. Both regular groups won, but the doors to the clubhouses had been opened considerably. Racial integration had become a reality in Du Pont politics.

Summary

A major organizational dilemma for neighborhood councils is the recruitment of slack resources. The Du Pont way of dealing with this dilemma was to approach it indirectly. There were few slack resources available from local businessmen to change the political structure; yet they paid for the ads that supported the *Du Pont News,* a major political resource of the council. There were few slack resources in the Italian Catholic churches for improving race relations; yet they were the mainstay of the Little League, which did more to improve race relations in the neighborhood than anything else. There were few slack resources in the regular political clubs to develop an urban-renewal plan; yet they threw their influence behind it.

The council's ability to recruit resources that would not have been committed as a result of direct appeals does in great measure account for its success. A direct appeal for resources implies that the exchange is simply time and effort for the reward of a new school, or better race relations, or a new park. For many groups and individuals in neighborhoods these rewards would not be sufficiently salient to make them enter an exchange process with a council. However, Du Pont offered the businessmen more business, the Catholic churches more activities with which to involve their parishioners, the regular clubs an opportunity to see that no one gained political advantage over them. They actually received the rewards they sought. The council, on the other hand, used the resources that these groups and individuals invested in ways other than they had intended.

Organizations are tangible, formal structures. However, they do not necessarily have to operate in direct, formal ways. Such procedures often raise costs beyond the level of rewards provided. At times organizations have to decide whether it is more important to control an aspect of community life or have everyone know that they control it.

NOTES

1. Robert A. Dahl, *Who Governs: Democracy and Power in an American City* (New Haven: Yale University Press, 1961), p. 307.
2. Ibid., p. 305.
3. *Du Pont News*, February 11, 1960, p. 1.
4. Ibid., May 2, 1958, p. 1.
5. Town Hall Meeting Committee Record, August 24, 1959.
6. Ibid., September 17, 1959.
7. Ibid.
8. *Du Pont News*, May 19, 1961, p. 1.
9. See Melvin M. Webber, "The Politics of Information," *Trans-action*, III (November-December 1965), 41–42.
10. See *Neighbors Unite for Better Communities: A Handbook on District Councils* (New York: United Community Funds and Councils of America, 1956), p. 2.
11. Dietrich C. Reitzes, "The Role of Organizational Structure: Union vs. Neighborhood in a Tension Situation," *Sociology: The Progress of a Decade*, ed. Seymour Lipset and Neil Smelser (Englewood Cliffs, N.J.: Prentice-Hall, 1961), p. 520.

Part III

Practice Problems

7

Community Organization
Workers

Interviews with members of the Du Pont Executive Committee
revealed that although over the years the council had developed a system of exchanges that enabled it to get the resources it needed to
achieve many of its goals, only in a few situations were any individuals
aware of the exchanges involved. None developed his awareness into
a generalized mode of operation. This part, "Practice Problems," deals
with the common problems of voluntary citizen organizations and
offers solutions derived from an exchange model of analysis. The major
responsibility for solving such organizational problems rests with staff
workers, who presumably are hired for such expertise.

Since its inception in 1956, Du Pont has had the services of a worker.
Each worker was a major resource of the council and provided, for
example, skill and expertise in a variety of areas, a ready source of
manpower, and a sense of commitment to the council's purposes. Since
the worker's salary was paid first by Jefferson House and then by
HEED, the council did not have to devote much of its resources to
fund-raising ventures. The investment of a worker in the council was
actually for the purpose of pump-priming on the part of HEED and
Jefferson House. Their ultimate hope was for the worker to help the
council develop so fully that it would become self-sufficient to the point
of either paying the worker's salary itself or being able to operate without a worker.

One of the functions of a worker, then, is to pyramid the resources of a council. From the examples noted in previous chapters, it is clear that Du Pont was successful in enlarging its supply of resources in a number of areas. Since there was agreement among council members that all four workers generally operated in similar fashion and since each was trained in the same school of social work, it is likely that an analysis of one worker's activities will typify the part that all the workers played in Du Pont's success.

Worker's Resources

What has held for other members of the council holds true for the worker: his statuses crucially affect actions taken. Martin Hill, the worker in 1962–1963, held three that were crucial in defining his activities: his status as a staff member of HEED, which paid his salary; his status as a staff worker for the citizen members of the Du Pont Neighborhood Council; his status as a member of the social work profession.

Determinants of the Worker's Activities

Hill was not completely under the control of any one of the groups concerned with how he did his job. Going along with the old adage "he who pays the piper calls the tune," one might expect that HEED, since it paid Hill's salary, exerted the crucial influence on what he did. There is no doubt that Hill paid considerable attention to the demands of HEED, but in many instances he responded to other pressures in deciding on courses of action and developed tactics that lessened the control HEED had over him. Du Pont itself was a potent source of power over HEED for Hill. For example, when Hill's supervisor at HEED put pressure on him to have Du Pont participate in a joint fund-raising campaign with HEED, Hill was able to say, with the backing of Du Pont's chairman, that the council was not interested. Actually, Hill was not interested either, since he had other fund-raising plans for Du Pont. Thus HEED did not have complete control over Hill, but it did set certain limits on him.

HEED. Each week Hill met with his supervisor to discuss the progress of his work, at which time it was made clear to him what was expected by his superiors. The criteria upon which Hill's supervisor judged his performance were: initiative and creativity; organization of work and the ability to plan ahead; effectiveness in forming sound relationships; ability to introduce issues and problems into the council and move the council toward their resolution; the ability to write and communicate succinctly.[1]

This supervisory conference reinforced the criteria of evaluation in the worker's mind. The achievement of specific goals, for example, getting a new school or starting a basketball league, was not one of the criteria. The primary standard of evaluation seemed to revolve around the worker's ability to involve people in working together on some problem. In this scheme people were much more central than solving problems. The real pressure on the worker was to get people into the council. For example, for Hill to keep his job, it was not necessary for the council to secure a new school, but it was necessary that people work on the problem of securing it.

Profession and ideology. Another factor that crucially affected how Hill did his job was his belief in grass-roots democracy. In another HEED council a dispute arose over whether a new school was needed or whether an old one could be renovated. When a delegation from the council conferred with the principal to demand a new school, the principal succeeded in convincing this group of middle-class women that renovation was the proper course. After the women had reported their feelings to the council, the worker, in private, told the researcher that they had been hoodwinked. Later he used his influence with people in the parents' association to have the issue placed on their next agenda. The worker's reasoning was that he was acting on the basis of what he felt the vast majority of the lower-class people in the neighborhood wanted.

This particular situation was typical of the way in which HEED staff workers saw themselves. Because they believed in a grass-roots ideology, they saw themselves as the spokesmen for the lower class—the people who did not join the council. Their belief that it is unfair for people to make decisions for others was the rationale for their actions. Their professional role of enabler notwithstanding, workers were quite willing to be directive and manipulative to press for low-income interests. Hill and his associates were in general agreement on the need for HEED and Du Pont to be responsive to lower-income needs. They believed that this responsiveness could only occur if lower-income people were in positions of leadership in HEED and the councils. In 1962–1963 this was not the case. Outside of the sports committee the vast majority of members were middle class (and of these only fifteen or twenty were to any degree active).

Members. A major problem for Hill was to get people involved in the council—to carry through on details, to plan, to take action, etc. Hill came to Du Pont in the fall of 1962 with the idea that his job was to be a catalyst in the neighborhood. His function, as he saw it, was to demonstrate what people could do for themselves and the neighborhood, and to provide an opportunity for them to do it. He soon found out, however, that even when people come to meetings, they do not necessarily want to involve themselves or assume responsibilities. Some members even seemed to view his presence as an opportunity of lessening their involvement. Such attitudes were a problem for Hill, for he was as concerned about how things got done as he was that they got done.

This disagreement in role definition of both member and worker was illustrated at a nominating committee meeting. The committee met and selected a slate of officers. The chairman asked the worker to call people and inform them of their selection. Hill reneged since he thought this job was the chairman's responsibility. He explained that he believed people would respond more favorably if they were called by the chairman. There were a few moments of tension because the chairman simply did not understand why the worker refused this job since the worker had been active in informally sounding people out for offices. Finally, there was a compromise. Hill and several committee members split the responsibility.

Hill reported privately that he was concerned about the lack of responsibility that he felt existed on the part of many key members of the council. Yet he could hardly say to the chairman, "I want you to be more responsible, and the way you will become more responsible is by following through on your decisions." The chairman considered

TABLE 2

What Is Your Opinion About the Worker's Job Performance?

$$(N = 61)$$

Response	Active Members	Sports Members	Other Members	Percentage
Superior	9	11	20	66%
Good	5	1	11	28
Average	1	1	—	3
Poor	1	1	—	3

NOTE: In this and subsequent tables "Active Members" refers to those whose combined attendance at two or more different committees' meetings totaled at least five. "Sports Members" refers to those who attended only sports committee meetings. "Other Members" refers to all others not categorized under the other two columns. See Appendix B, "Schedule for Interviewing Council Participants."

himself responsible. Since he was concerned only about getting things done, he felt that his request was legitimate. He had a limited amount of time. Besides, "what was the worker being paid for anyway?" He considered Hill's role to be that of an executive secretary.

There were a number of reasons why Hill did not clearly draw certain lines about his role. First, he soon realized that he had to gain the confidence and cooperation of the council members if he were to involve them to the fullest extent. One way to win their trust was to give evidence of hard work. In part, by writing letters, arranging for meetings, and contacting officials, he gained the membership's confidence, but he also set work patterns for himself that were difficult to change. As table 2 illustrates, Hill was successful in gaining the confidence of the membership.

Secondly, and more important, Du Pont was not an organization with an unlimited amount of resources. If the worker refused to do something and a failure resulted, the council could be severely weakened. Thus, Hill confided, the decision about whether he should or should not do things had to be decided on the specifics of each situation. In addition, his predecessors had set certain precedents. Members had certain expectations of workers. Although table 3 illustrates that these expectations differed considerably, a majority of respondents viewed the worker as someone who expedited the work of the council not only by coordinating, but by actually doing the legwork and helping out with the work when members were unavailable or unable to do it. One respondent said, "It's friendliness; it feels like cooperation;

TABLE 3

What Should the Worker Do?

(N = 68)

Response	Percentage
Expedite by helping out	41%
Advise on ways of solving neighborhood problems	41
Expedite by coordinating others	25
Recruit people and groups	18
Serve as a link with governmental and other organizations	16
Give emotional support to sustain participation	13
Enable members to engage in process	4
Develop leaders	3
Others	3

NOTE: Totals add to more than 100% due to the possibility of multiple coding. See Appendix B, "Schedule for Interviewing Council Participants."

it's bad to have someone say, 'Oh, no, I can't do that, it's not my job.' "
The more sophisticated members might have said it differently, but
essentially they felt that it was he who worked for them, and not
vice versa.

The consequence of Hill's not clearly delineating his role was that he
had little time for the work he wanted to do. He would have liked to
visit meetings of local groups and devote time to educational problems.
Yet he found himself bogged down in following up on details for committees. Instead of functioning as a leader or an enabler, more often
than not, he found himself acting like a member's helper. Table 4
breaks down into hours the worker's typical week.

TABLE 4
Worker's Typical Weekly Schedule

Activity	Hours
Attending committee meetings	8
Preparing for meetings: agendas, conferences with chairmen, meeting notices	8
Following up on meetings and ongoing council programs	16
Attending supervisory conference and staff meetings; miscellaneous	6
Total	38

NOTE: This table was derived from a time card kept by Hill for three weeks.

Nevertheless, Hill was neither completely under the control of the
members, nor at the mercy of HEED. On the other hand, neither was
he completely free to follow his personal ideology or professional standards of practice in the utilization of his resources. He was forced to
develop tactics to steer his way through these competing pressures to
achieve his ends or rewards.

Utilization of the Worker's Resources

Hill listed in order of importance those rewards which he received
from his work at Du Pont. These included: (1) having a sense of
accomplishment when a project had been carried through to completion; (2) seeing individuals grow and develop through council participation; (3) seeing the council develop a "fight city hall" attitude; (4)
overcoming obstacles such as the sports committee's hostility; (5) finding opportunities to foster the programs and the goals he thought were
important.[2] To achieve these rewards, Hill utilized his resources in
specific ways:

Program stimulator. The constant pressure on the worker to involve people in the council tended to make Hill promote programs that he felt people would be interested in, and then keep very close watch on these programs lest they fail and interest diminish. Since the ultimate constraint on Hill was the fear that the council would not survive, he was always prepared with suggestions for programs.[3] Hill's concern about programs was highlighted in his first real speech to the council at the first general meeting he attended. To the amazement of the older members, he rattled off seven new projects:

Hill's first comment was about the traffic sign at Market and Cherry. . . . He next mentioned the lack of space for an office at Jefferson House and the need for one in the area. There was the problem of raising money for it. The area around the dock is to be redeveloped and the area around Flatiron Bridge South is due for new housing. The Council would probably want to keep abreast of these problems. . . . There was also a lot for the Health Committee to do. There was the possibility of a blood bank.[4]

Informal director. According to an enabler's role, a worker may suggest programs, may point out alternatives and possible consequences, but may not actually make decisions. This role is similar to that of a therapist who, after helping a patient see the ramifications of a problem, lets the patient make the decisions on the assumption that self-determination is therapy in itself. The therapist must be able to let the patient make up his own mind, even if his decision is to leave therapy. Hill was clearly unable to let the council die if he were to achieve any of his professional goals, let alone retain his job. Thus to keep the council alive, as well as to achieve his own ends, he was forced to assume a great deal of control over council activities.

It is true that he never voted and almost never publicly stated which course of action should be taken, unless opinion was requested. Yet in actuality, in informal and subtle ways, he decided to a large extent what should be done. On almost all occasions he conferred with the committee chairmen before meetings. At these conferences agendas were set, possible projects were discussed, and general agreement on strategy secured. Frequently on these occasions the worker stated what he thought should and should not be done.

Even at meetings Hill controlled to a great degree what occurred. It was usually clear what he thought about a particular project. When he disagreed, he asked questions that implied that the project was not such a good idea or perhaps the timing was wrong. Even his facial expressions indicated his preference. He generally shared the enthusiasm of the group about particular projects and often said openly that certain projects and ideas were good. Withholding his approval and enthusiasm was a potent source of control that often made a committee continue discussions and change its plans.

Bargainer. On another level Hill bargained with members. He was dependent on their approval of whatever he did. Since he was a paid worker, it was difficult for him not to act in accordance with their expectations.

Many members of the sports committee originally were hostile to the worker, for they openly disapproved of anyone being paid to do what they did for nothing.[5] It took almost four months of weekly meetings before Hill made his first suggestion at a sports committee meeting. Prior to that time he had merely taken minutes and served as a secretary, a function he disliked. The following paragraphs describe his developing relationship with the committee (the second was written four months after the first):

The worker seemed to be completely passive at this meeting, almost immobilized by the amount of hostility in general and the implied criticism of his work. He volunteered some information about the possibility of other agencies giving the committee space for meeting if they disaffiliated. It was almost as if he was intimidated.[6]

The worker made his first suggestion of the year at this meeting when he said "well perhaps it would be best if we just forgot about the parade this year and make sure that it doesn't happen again next year," referring to the gate crashers. He functioned once again as the minute taker, and rereader of motions. Yet there was a definite change in the members' relationship to him.[7]

Hill's activities in this committee illustrate the way in which he bargained to achieve his ends. He pursued a policy of doing what the committee wanted until his acceptance had been won. After the May 14 meeting he gradually began to make additional suggestions. He stopped attending all the meetings; and when he did come, he no longer took the minutes. Hill believed his time should be put to better use in housing and educational matters. Early in May he formed an informal alliance with the most influential member of the sports committee, who wanted to be and was elected council chairman. Hill wrote:

Contact with Mr. [M.]. We met at the Board of Estimate hearings where he was testifying. He will accept chairmanship. Discussed possibility of Chatham Green South as a sports-recreation complex. He was very enthused.[8]

With the sanction of the new chairman, Hill was able to stop going to every sports committee meeting. Through bargaining he had achieved his goal—he had exchanged support for the chairmanship for less investment of his own resources in the sports committee.

Backstop and prodder. Once a project was decided upon, Hill involved himself in it completely. As table 5 indicates, twice as many contacts were originated by the worker than by the members.

TABLE 5
Contacts with Members Outside of Meetings
(N=309)

Contacts	Number
Member-originated	103
Worker-originated	206

NOTE: This table was derived from the Worker's Log (see Appendix D). The number of chance contacts was negligible. A contact is defined as a personal meeting, phone call, or written communication.

Since Hill realized that success or failure of a project would have vital effects on the council, he tended to play two distinct roles. First of all he was a backstop. In other words, if the education chairman did not write an article for the newspaper, the worker met the deadline. As noted earlier, there was a tendency to slough off work on the worker simply because he was always there. Hill disliked this attitude because he took it as a sure sign of lack of commitment on the part of members. However, reports like the following were common:

Two ladies who submitted articles for their churches came along with Frieda [R.] and brought coffee and cake. They read galleys, counted words and seemed to be satisfied. . . . The worker performed no function other than writing articles people hadn't written for one reason or another.[9]

TABLE 6
Worker-originated Contacts with Members Outside of Meetings
(N=206)

Contacts	Number
To check on or secure task performance	138
To share general information	68

To avoid this role, Hill was forced to become a prodder. Table 6 indicates that he spent a great deal of effort checking up on people to make sure that they had accepted and followed through on assignments. He often tried to get the committee chairmen to do this task, but in most cases he found himself playing backstop for them.

Worker's Effect on the Council

Although it was not possible to collect information systematically on contacts between members outside of meetings, from observation of the council and discussions with members, it is clear that communication outside of meetings was probably carried on more from worker to member and vice versa than from member to member. Hill was certainly the key figure in Du Pont's communication network. He received the incoming mail and read it before telephoning the appropriate committee chairman. Hill knew more about the council, and influenced it more, than anyone else.[10]

Functional Effects

Hill was aiming for a time when he would not have to push and backstop, constantly suggest programs, and be responsible for every aspect of council functioning. Neither he nor his predecessors ever realized this utopia in Du Pont. Yet their presence and activities were vital in Du Pont's development and successes. Each provided the council with resources that enhanced its ability to enter into favorable exchanges. The pushing and the backstopping tended to keep an individual's costs from outweighing his rewards and thus maintained participation. Of equal significance for the council was the expertise of the worker in particular program areas. The Urban Renewal Plan was mainly the result of the efforts of the second staff worker; the Little League overcame its initial growing pains from the dedication to and the knowledge of sports of the first worker; the reading improvement program grew because of Hill's interest. A new worker served the council at approximately two-year intervals. Each pumped new resources into it since each had somewhat different interests and concerns.

Each worker provided the council with a great source of emotional rewards. Hill knew everyone. He was friendly. If someone was sick or had a death in the family, he sent a card. When others were discouraged to the point of quitting, he sparked the enthusiasm to continue the fight. The fact that he was concerned enough to call someone about a meeting lent a certain amount of importance to the person's attendance —the individual felt needed. The answers of respondents to the question about the quality of Hill's job performance indicate the expressive function the worker played. One respondent said: "He's very nice to meet at meetings and in the street. It makes one want to attend meetings to be greeted so nicely." Another member said about one of Hill's predecessors: "Oh yes, Danny, he seemed like he cared so much but yet was such a little boy. I just couldn't help but want to get out and help him."

Another vital function the worker performed was keeping the council going. People lost interest, moved out of the neighborhood, became ill, etc., but the worker carried on. This sense of stability and continuity was particularly important in dealing with city departments. A high official of the borough president's office stated at a HEED conference on neighborhood councils that it is the staff that makes a council effective. Perhaps city agencies attached significance to council staff because their presence implied that an organization was not going to disappear and their efforts with it would not be wasted—or perhaps because city officials preferred to negotiate with other professionals, or merely because the worker was accessible on a day-by-day basis.

Dysfunctional Effects

The professionally trained community organizers at HEED agreed that a staff worker was vital for a council. Their point of view was that the more skilled a staff worker, the better the council. Without such a belief staff workers doubtless could not have done their job with great commitment and enthusiasm. The idea that their presence was dysfunctional in some respects did not concern them.[11] Table 7 indicates that this concept did not concern members either.

TABLE 7
Is a Professional Social Worker Necessary?
(N=65)

Response	Percentage
Yes	75%
No	14
Not sure	11

NOTE: The responses of members who were agency and church professional staff workers are not included in the above table. Only one of them considered a professional worker unnecessary. A professional worker was interpreted to respondents to

Without a worker a council would have to develop some mechanism or mechanisms to ensure that work would be completed. Committee chairmen might be forced into this role. If they were, certainly the costs of their participation would rise. Undoubtedly the organization would also be forced to devise additional means of getting work done, such as increasing the commitment of members, developing informal sources of compliance, or developing more potent means of socialization. The presence of a worker obviated the necessity for these alternatives. He lowered the costs of participation, making it possible for all participants to maximize their rewards without paying a full organizational price.

Tension reduction. If the worker were withdrawn, it would be questionable whether or not Du Pont could survive because of the worker's effects on vital organizational processes. Take, for example, the following situation: by January of 1963, Hill had been with Du Pont for four months. In that time he had worked diligently to ensure that council committees moved ahead. Yet there was noticeable apathy. He was not sure what the problem was; but since he was new at his job and obviously threatened, he increased his efforts to encourage people to attend meetings and become involved with the council. The problem was finally verbalized at an executive committee meeting:

Harry [W.] stated that the Council is losing its identity. He criticized the worker for sending out too many flyers to people who really weren't concerned with the Council and for not picking up the mail and perhaps for not mailing out letters that were supposed to have been mailed out.[12]

There was a positive result. The aftermath of this charge was a heated debate and a dramatic change in the attitude of those present. (Hill remained silent throughout.) The charges seemed to draw everyone together and served to increase solidarity rather than pull the council apart. New ideas suddenly emerged, and the meeting was carried on with great enthusiasm.

The natural reluctance of Hill to initiate such discussions until he had exhausted his efforts had tended to postpone the manifestations of member dissatisfactions. His activities had kept tension from erupting with the force or intensity it might have had had he not been present.

---

mean a professional social worker. Unfortunately, respondents were not probed to see if they had a clear concept of a professional social worker. Therefore, some positive responses may refer only to the belief that a full-time person is necessary. See Appendix B, "Schedule for Interviewing Council Participants."

Members had not been following through on their assignments, yet the burden had not fallen on others. This reduction of tension can prevent a council from really taking stock of such predicaments and asking such questions as, "What do we have to do?" "Is it really worth it?" and "How can we deal with it?"

The possibility of a council's strengthening itself by dealing with its tensions and problems is lessened by the presence of the worker because his activities tend to alleviate the problems. It is possible that death comes to many councils because the commitment and the solidarity necessary to overcome major organizational problems never develop in the course of dealing with minor problems. Workers take care of the minor problems simply because they are afraid the council might not survive otherwise.[13]

Diminishment of solidarity. There are other consequences of the worker's presence. For example, the offices of recording and corresponding secretary in Du Pont were filled at each election, but the secretaries never functioned because the worker performed these roles. Members simply allowed their names to be used. Writing minutes, sending meeting notices, preparing agendas, and drafting letters were not the most rewarding of tasks. Many organizations handle this lack of rewards in these vital functions by making the secretariat a stepping stone or proving ground for the presidency, thus immeasurably increasing the attractiveness of the job. This mechanism did not develop in Du Pont because of the worker's presence.

TABLE 8

What Would Occur to Du Pont if the Worker Were Withdrawn?

(N=74)

Response	Percentage
Collapse	32%
Be severely curtailed	42
Stay together	12
Do better	3
Not sure	10

NOTE: See Appendix B, "Schedule for Interviewing Council Participants."

The argument is often advanced that by taking care of the details, the worker releases participants' energy for more vital activities. In Du Pont it is questionable whether in the long run this released energy redounded to the council's benefit. Table 8 indicates that most members felt the council would be severely curtailed or collapse without a worker. Thus the energy the worker released did not increase the self-reliance or solidarity of members. It may be hypothesized that the worker's presence tends to weaken the participants' sense of value or usefulness in many council activities and thereby lessens the possibility of developing solidarity.[14]

The sports committee displayed the most solidarity of any committee in the council. It also demanded the greatest expenditure of time and energy. A great part of its success was due to the fact that each member realized the Little League could not function without him. It was not possible for Hill to backstop every member. Unless each person did his job, there would be no Little League. The individual was needed. However, a member only had to be in Du Pont for a short time to see that many of its other activities could be carried on without him. This knowledge made solidarity difficult to achieve because the rewards for performing tasks were diminished.

Lessening of commitment. As table 9 indicates, Hill had almost as many contacts with non-members between meetings as with members.

TABLE 9
Worker's Contacts Outside of Meetings
(N=581)

Contacts	Number
With members	309
With nonmembers	272

NOTE: See Appendix D, "Worker's Log." Letters received from nonmember sources were not recorded by Hill. Their inclusion would substantially increase the nonmember contacts.

By virtue of his presence, he initiated or followed upon almost all contacts with outside organizations and was the first to receive their return communications. Since this procedure forced committee chairmen and members to communicate with him, they did not have to communicate as often with one another. The less contact the members had among themselves, the more segmented their council participation tended to become. This problem was intensified since committee members seldom attended general meetings of the total council. As the situation existed in Du Pont, the sports committee members were concerned with sports, the health committee with health, etc. Opportunities for developing informal council relationships were restricted, the chances of commitment to the total organization were lessened, and dependence on the worker increased.[15]

Had the worker not been present, Du Pont would have been forced to develop a new way of coordinating its activities. It is doubtful if an unpaid chairman could have handled all the work that had to be done. Many of the committees might have been consolidated; the offices of recording and corresponding secretary might have become real rather than in name only. The executive committee would have had to struggle to secure the resources that the worker invested.

With a worker it was possible for the executive committee to convene once a month at a meeting arranged by the worker, make whatever decisions and plans had to be made, and sit back with the assurance that all would be taken care of with a minimum of concern required of them as a group. Without the worker this complacency could not exist. An organization in which members send out meeting notices, write minutes, contact outside organizations, and carry out all activities by themselves would probably also choose different programs than those supplied by a worker with considerable resources to implement his ideas. At the least, such an organization would have to depend heavily on the commitment of its members.

Summary

It would be difficult to argue with Hill and his predecessors' contention that they were vital factors in Du Pont's success. They supplied the council with many of the resources it needed to promote its programs. In addition, Hill was aware that members tended to assume less of their responsibility as long as he was there, that only a very few were committed to the council, that important segments of the neighborhood were not represented, and that the council was, in general, too dependent on him. Yet, in the main, he was unable to deal with these problems. The fact that he and his predecessors contributed in part to some of the problems does not mean that workers cannot develop effective ways to deal with them. The following chapters will explore a number of possible solutions to these organizational problems.

NOTES

1. These criteria were stated in an interview with Hill's supervisor. He did not rate them in order of importance.
2. This data was recorded in a personal interview with Hill.

3. There is no intent to claim that the actions described in this section occur inevitably in all councils or that they could not be controlled. The intent is merely to point out the conditions that constrain workers in the direction of these actions.

4. Du Pont General Meeting field notes, October 18, 1962.

5. This opinion changed to one of approval after the most influential member of the committee was elected council chairman. See table 1.

6. Du Pont Sports Committee field notes, January 22, 1963.

7. Ibid., May 14, 1963.

8. Staff Worker's Log, May 3, 1963. Hill kept a log of all his activities outside of meetings for approximately four months. See Appendix D, "Worker's Log." It should be recognized that keeping the log was a burdensome, time-consuming task for Hill. The logs were collected from him on a weekly basis. He admitted that there were times when he was more meticulous than others in filling them out.

9. Du Pont Newspaper Committee field notes, May 23, 1963.

10. For a discussion of the relationship between centrality in a group's communication network and power in a group, see Terence K. Hopkins, *The Exercise of Influence in Small Groups* (Totowa, N.J.: Bedminster Press, 1964), pp. 28–29.

11. This idea was actually mentioned by an untrained worker at one of HEED's staff meetings. No one picked it up as worthy of discussion. "Dysfunctional" in this section refers to those activities of the worker which do not add to a council's ability to pyramid its resources.

12. Du Pont Executive Committee field notes, January 9, 1963.

13. It could be argued that Hill's reluctance to discuss council apathy was simply an example of poor practice in that he was not aware or skilled in the positive use of conflict or tension to achieve goals. On the other hand, it can be argued even with skill that the constraint on a worker to prove his mettle and keep a council going would at the least affect his timing in the use of conflict and at the most would postpone his dealing with tensions until the damage done was irreparable.

14. In discussing the one stable council he investigated in St. Louis, Mo., Sridharan notes: "Indeed, this was the only council that did not advance lack of leadership as a factor hampering movement. . . . Yet another interesting point was brought out by the conference leaders when they suggested that if they had a full time, paid, professional staff worker right from the beginning, there was a good chance of the people in the area developing too much of a dependence on him and thereby showing an unwillingness to assume any type of responsibility" (K. V. Sridharan, "Area Approach to Social Welfare Planning," [Ph.D. diss., Ohio State University, 1959], p. 69).

15. For a discussion of the dangers of segmentalized participation and the concomitant strains toward functional autonomy in organizations, see Alvin W. Gouldner, "Organizational Analysis," *Sociology Today*, ed. Robert K. Merton et al. (New York: Basic Books, 1959), p. 417.

8

Individual Participation

IN THE Du Pont area there were approximately seventy-five hundred adults who might have attended council meetings. In 1962–1963 year, which was typical of most other years, only 125 or 1.7 percent of the adult population attended at least one meeting. Outside of the sports committee only thirty-four people attended three or more meetings. See table 10.

TABLE 10

Attendance at Du Pont, 1962–1963

(N=125)

	Members Attending
Committees (other than sports)	
One meeting only	44
Two meetings only (of one or more committees)	17
Three or more meetings (of one or more committees)	34
Total	95
Sports committee	
One or two meetings	7
Three or more meetings	23
Total	30

This relatively small number of participants was a source of concern to Hill, partly because he believed in grass-roots democracy and partly because lack of participation hampered the council's operation. Nothing seemed more demoralizing than having only the committee chairman and one or two members come to a meeting. In such situations little could be accomplished since there were not enough people to act or discuss. Members also felt that lack of participation was the major problem in the council.

However, a large membership is not necessarily a *sine qua non* of a council's successful goal attainment. Du Pont managed to accomplish a great deal with a small, active membership. One informant summed up this ability by exclaiming, "I am amazed at how much a few people can do!" However, it cannot be denied that many projects were not undertaken because of lack of participation. Besides, from the point of view that one function of Du Pont was to educate through participation, regular attendance was a requisite. Thus an analysis of the determinants of participation in Du Pont is a matter of considerable professional concern.

The Participation Exchange

The participants in Du Pont differed in significant ways from the general population of the area. Jews were clearly overrepresented, Chinese and Puerto Ricans underrepresented. The council was made up of a group of people in an income bracket that was much higher than the average neighborhood income. Approximately three out of four council participants were high school graduates. Only one out of four neighborhood residents had graduated from high school. Interviews revealed that council participants tended to be more upwardly mobile than nonparticipants; they also were more prone to taking risks in relation to their employment. In general, the Du Pont participant emerged as better educated, higher paid, more upwardly mobile, and less concerned about job security than the average neighborhood resident.

Class-determined Rewards

The profile of a Du Pont participant was that of middle rather than working and lower class.[1] In a neighborhood that was preponderantly working and lower class in makeup, the council tended to be preponderantly middle class.[2]

Foskett notes that one of the most basic and significant facts about social participation is that it is not uniformly distributed throughout the population but tends to be concentrated in a minority of citizens. Since some people have more contact with others, especially leaders, they are structurally well placed to participate, that is, shopkeepers have an advantage over mill hands. Some people are better equipped to communicate their ideas; they possess the social skills needed for participation.[3] Du Pont's middle-class makeup corroborates the findings of many studies that the working and lower class is significantly underrepresented in voluntary organizations.

What may be implied from Foskett and others is that for lower- and working-class people the costs of community participation generally outweigh the rewards. Whatever risk is involved is greater for them because they could lose what little they have, and because of this risk, community participation involves a higher cost. They often do not possess the time, money, or even the clothes necessary to participate in community organizations. Fact-finding, delegations, and drawn-out deliberations are not direct or fast enough and, therefore, frustrating. In addition, potential future rewards, such as better housing or better sanitation, are often not highly salient for them.

Although these ideas about the middle-class nature of council-like organizations seem to offer a ready explanation for the participation figures in Du Pont, one cannot assume that the council could not have achieved a larger rate of participation from the working and lower class. Table 11 notes that a substantial portion of the working- and lower-class population indicated a readiness to join a community organization to improve the neighborhood. Secondly, the sports committee

TABLE 11

Willingness of Working- and Lower-Class Residents
to Join a Community-Improvement Organization
(N=788)

Response	Percentage
Probably would	50%
Probably would not	43
Not sure, do not know	7

SOURCE: Table was derived from *Codebook, Adult Survey,* vol. I (New York: Mobilization for Youth, 1962), p. 8.

was mainly working class. Its success depended upon the availability of opportunities for working-class men to perform nonverbal as well as verbal acts vital to the functioning of a program. The procedures of the sports committee were such that the rewards were not cancelled out by the costs and were available to any working-class member, since the resources required were in his possession. This balance did not exist in other committees where considerable organizational knowledge, verbal facility, and technical expertise were required.

When asked why he was not active in other committees, one member of the sports committee said: "Well, as you can see, most of us aren't very educated. We didn't feel that we could do much in housing, but with baseball . . . well, we could do that." From the researcher's point of view, this respondent was an intelligent, capable person; yet his perception of himself as a member of a less educated class determined where he would invest his resources and what rewards he would seek. It can be hypothesized that the more often a council can offer rewards congruent with those dictated by an individual's status as a member of a social class, the more members of that class will join the council.[4] The differences between middle-class and working- and lower-class patterns and interests make it difficult to maintain these classes in one organization. Du Pont's ability to involve both was a major organizational achievement.

A community organizer who desires to involve various classes within one organization has to provide opportunities for the meaningful investment of resources aside from the verbal and highly technical kinds. Such opportunities exist in volunteer fire departments, mass rallies, parades, cooperatives, etc. Once working-class individuals are involved, there is at least the possibility of changing the perceptions that limit their participation. Unfortunately, in Du Pont most of the staff workers paid as little attention to the sports committee as possible. They did not make use of the opportunity to broaden the participation of intelligent members such as the one previously quoted.

Ethnically Determined Rewards

The most striking point about the membership statistics in table 12 is the overrepresentation of Italians on the sports committee and Jews on other committees. As has already been noted, the sports committee was set up so that the Italian churches could maintain control over their own boys and keep them in the church. The Italians were concerned with the Italian Catholic community, and the sports committee enabled Italian participants to act in accordance with this concern. On the other hand, it is no surprise that the Italians were underrepresented on other council committees. First, they had no tradition of participation in community affairs with a group viewed as an outsider.[5] Secondly, the association of the council with Jefferson House—from which Italians felt driven—as well as with the Protestant clergy, gave Du Pont a negative image with the Italians. And thirdly, the Italians viewed the political clubs as the legitimate groups for dealing with neighborhood affairs. Therefore, in committees other than the sports committee, there were considerable costs to an Italian in his ethnic status.

TABLE 12
Ethnicity of Du Pont Participants, 1962–1963

	Sports Committee Percentage (N=30)	Other Committees Percentage (N=95)
Italians	54%	10%
Jews	7	37
Negroes	23	13
Puerto Ricans	13	8
Chinese	0	1
Others	3	31

Jews were not only active in the council but also in the parents' associations and political clubs. As noted in an earlier chapter, Jews in Du Pont had the feeling that community affairs were vital to them. It was several Jewish mothers who originated the concern with the quality of the schools. They wanted their children to be prepared for college and felt threatened by the evident deterioration of the local schools. The council was the mechanism through which they handled these threats. Also, the lack of any Jewish religious or community organizations of any substance in Du Pont made those Jews inclined to organizational activity more likely to join the council.

None of the six Puerto Ricans who attended meetings—outside of the sports committee—came more than once. Although the council offered rewards to Jews and Italians as members of their group by the choice of certain projects, such as improving the schools and setting up a Little League, it did not offer similar rewards to Puerto Ricans. As noted, the Puerto Rican desire for a meeting place was not viewed as an appropriate council concern.

Although Negroes and Puerto Ricans faced similar problems regarding jobs, housing, and discrimination, there were significant differences in their situations. Politically, as noted in an earlier chapter, the neighborhood had come alive for the Negro. Prior to 1962, his vote had not been in demand, but the primary fights in both parties were giving him a chance for recognition. The Reform Democrats fared poorly in campaigning on issues responsive to Negro concerns; however, the insurgent Republicans, made up of the most politically conservative elements in the neighborhood, did surprisingly well. Their leader sought out influential Negroes as precinct captains and, in general, sought their personal support. The results reinforce the view held by several informants that Negroes want to be represented by their own no matter what the issue.

The value of education was of increasing concern to Negro parents; their participation in the parents' associations was steadily increasing. The Negroes who were active in council activities participated quite fully. A Negro woman was chosen chairman of the education committee, to fill the unexpired term of a Jewish chairman who resigned; a Negro man was elected second vice-president of the council for 1964. The desire of Negroes, as a group, to be accepted into existing organizations has been met, by and large, by the council.

Chinese children played with other children in the neighborhood and attended the local public schools, but Du Pont was merely a dormitory for Chinese adults. The council created no other rewards for them than the Little League. It had contact with only one Chinese adult during the year of observation and had little awareness about what this ethnic group desired for itself.

This discussion clearly shows that a council can create situations that are rewarding by virtue of an individual's status as a member of an ethnic group. However, not all groups are like the Jewish group, which has a tradition of community participation and is, therefore, able to create its own rewards in community groups. It took clear thinking on the part of the council's leadership to involve Italians, by creating the rewards they desired as a group, that is, by maintaining the solidarity of their community.

Individual members of the council were aware of the way the Italian community had been brought into the council. Yet in the numerous discussions about the lack of membership, it was never suggested that the Chinese and Puerto Rican communities could be approached by using the same technique.[6] One reason for this failure was the idea that a council was an organization to bring all groups together to work on some common problem. However, some groups had problems that were peculiar to themselves. For example, the Chinese women were anxious to learn English. It is easy to speculate on the potential gains in participation that might have accrued to the council had it offered assistance in this endeavor.

Maximization of Rewards

One possible explanation for the discrepancy between the actual and the potential participation in Du Pont is suggested by Ward Goodenough:

Competition between their several wants forces people to make choices leading to the formation of scales of preference and relative value. People try to devise modes of action having a high net efficacy. So it is, that many of the customary activities in which we engage are able to gratify not one but a number of our wants. And by limiting the occasions when we engage in them to those times when we experience the many wants they are capable of gratifying, *we maximize the rewards* [emphasis added] to be derived from them. One need only think, for example, of the wants that giving a dinner party in our own society may help to gratify, such as being with congenial or stimulating people, paying one's social debts, impressing a business client, indulging one's appetite for drink and good food, getting the house thoroughly cleaned, etc.[7]

Thus those interested in community improvement could have pursued this interest in other organizations that offered better possibilities for maximizing rewards. Kiwanis clubs offer community-service rewards, as do mothers' clubs, sisterhoods, sodalities, holy name societies, American Legion posts, etc. These also offer a range of other emotional, ideological, and negotiable rewards related to the varied statuses people occupy. The implication for recruitment here is clear. If councils make their recruitment appeals on the basis of community-betterment projects or service rewards, as is often done, they must consider the convertibility of these service rewards to ideological, emotional, and negotiable rewards.

There is much evidence that the ability to maximize rewards is one or more of their statuses was a significant factor for Du Pont's participants. The reports of members in table 13 reveal that it was not the projects alone that kept them active. Even though there is some disagreement between the two coders, emotional rewards were clearly important to participants. Responses in this category centered around the satisfaction related to meeting people, making friends, and enjoying council procedures, such as listening to discussions or publishing a newspaper.[8]

TABLE 13
Self-Report of Rewards Received by Participants
(N=81)

| | Percentage of Individuals Obtaining | | | |
	Ideological Rewards	Service Rewards	Emotional Rewards	Negotiable Rewards
Coder I	12%	54%	52%	4%
Coder II	12	41	43	5

NOTE: See Appendix B, "Schedule for Interviewing Council Participants." Since this question was open-ended and the responses had to be coded into a typology, two independent coders were used as a check on the reliability of the interpretation of responses. Definitions of the various reward categories conform to those given in Chapter 2. Totals add to more than 100% due to multiple coding.

From a common-sense viewpoint, as well as from observing the council's participants, it was to be expected that the members would in some measure derive emotional rewards from their participation. On the other hand, the low percentage reporting negotiable rewards is surprising. It is likely that either the respondents felt that negotiable rewards are illegitimate exchanges for their investment of resources, or they were unaware of receiving them. However, there is much evidence of the presence of negotiable rewards: the social workers and the ministers enhanced their own organizations and their professional careers through their council activities. One even wrote a book about church participation in neighborhood affairs. One of the housewives launched a political career based on the reputation she developed in the council. One of the politicians received the Republican nomination for state senator shortly after completing his term as chairman. Another politician functioned as the unofficial emissary of his political club.

It can be hypothesized that the more statuses an individual occupies in which a council's rewards are salient, the more likely he is to participate in the council. The people who were highly involved in Du Pont were those who tended also to occupy statuses of minister, social worker, and politician. (See table 14.) All received negotiable rewards for use in their professional status systems. Du Pont was less successful in offering negotiable rewards to working- and lower-class participants. This failure may be due in part to the circumscribed nature of their jobs and the limited number of other systems in which they participate.

TABLE 14
Occupations of Du Pont's Executive Committee, 1962–1963
(N=16)

Occupation	Number of Members
Minister	4
Politician	4
Social worker	3
Businessman	2
Housewife	2
Bridge worker (former union organizer)	1

The Salient Reward

Although maximizing rewards is clearly related to participation, it cannot be concluded that people join a council expressly for maximizing any and all rewards. Certainly some rewards are much more salient than others for participants. The problem for Hill was first to discover what the salient rewards were, and then to devise specific means for involving people in council activities that would bring them these rewards. Neither task was easy.

TABLE 15
Problems That Participants Considered Appropriate to Bring to Du Pont
(N=69)

Problem	Percentage
Parks and recreation	98%
Interracial relationships	87
Teen-age behavior	87
School facilities	81
Pleasant living conditions	46
Family relationships	15
Employment	15
Friendship opportunities	13
Personal or family health	12

NOTE: See Appendix B, "Schedule for Interviewing Council Participants." Total adds to more than 100% due to multiple coding.

It would seem logical that the most salient rewards for individuals would relate to family relationships, a good job, personal and family health, opportunity to make friends, and pleasant living conditions; however, table 15 indicates that it is precisely in these areas that Du Pont participants did not view the council as an appropriate place to take their problems. The problems left for the council were those which in noncrisis situations would include the less salient rewards. Thus a council can be expected to have difficulty offering salient rewards in noncrisis situations. This difficulty may account for Du Pont's dependency on organizational ties and friendship bonds to get participants to attend.[9] See table 16.

TABLE 16
How Participants Became Involved in Du Pont
(N=87)

Initial Involvement	Percentage
Sent as an organizational representative	66%
Invited by a friend	18
Attended alone, out of civic interest	16

NOTE: See Appendix B, "Schedule for Interviewing Council Participants.

Identification of Rewards

The methods used in Du Pont to discover the rewards that potential participants might be seeking often did not adequately deal with the key question of saliency. The following methods were attempted:

Surveys. Du Pont conducted several surveys of community needs during the years of its existence. None seemed to have any important effect on either the council or the neighborhood. There were several reasons: these surveys were centered on discovering the problems in the neighborhood that people perceived or the services that they desired. Respondents were asked to rate a list of potential problems similar to those in table 17. The assumption was that council efforts to solve the problem with the highest rating would present the most salient rewards. This was not necessarily true. In the first place, the responses were generally interpreted in terms of services needed. Yet many observers have noted that people living in slum areas are not so concerned with the improvement of housing and other facilities as they are with maintaining their self-esteem.[10] Services are tangible and easily lend themselves to council planning and action. Emotions are considerably less tangible or amenable to planning and action. The surveys that Du Pont took did not really tap the emotional needs of respondents.

TABLE 17

What in Your Opinion Is the Biggest Problem Around Here?

Transportation
Public schools
City police protection
Teen-age behavior
Behavior of certain racial groups

NOTE: This question was asked of residents of the Du Pont neighborhood. See *Codebook, Adult Survey,* vol. I (New York: Mobilization for Youth, 1962), p. 5.

Secondly, as table 17 illustrates, the Du Pont surveys tended to gather information about general problems that affect everyone in the neighborhood. They did not gather information about what specific segments or groups in the neighborhood wanted for themselves. As noted earlier, rewards related to such desires are often the most salient for group members.

Meeting attendants. Du Pont did not take any surveys during 1962–1963. Several other methods, which were even less adequate than the surveys, evolved for discovering salient rewards. One was to let people who attended meetings determine the rewards that the council should offer simply on the basis of what they thought the neighborhood needed. The problem with this method lies in the limited knowledge of most people and in the fact that different groups actually want different things. The middle class may want more middle-income housing, the lower class more low-income housing. When those who attend council meetings have substantially different interests than those of the majority of residents, the chances are likely that the council will not offer rewards salient to the majority of residents.

Committee structure. Another reason why Du Pont did not always offer the most salient rewards lay in the formal structure of council committees. Chairmen felt compelled to promote activities in their committees. Once there was a health committee, there was a constraint to have programs in health whether these offered salient rewards or not. As a result, the health committee found itself in the somewhat ludicrous position of having almost twice as many projects as people in attendance at meetings.

The worker. Hill was extremely concerned about finding out what salient rewards the people wanted. Overburdened with administrative details that left him little time to study the neighborhood, he used the basic technique of the general meeting as a means of determining the saliency of a project. For example, for the February 1963 general meeting, he saturated the neighborhood with announcements about a speaker on consumer fraud. The number of people who came to the meeting and the degree of interest they displayed were taken as indicators of the saliency of the rewards involved. Few people came and consumer fraud was not discussed again. Yet it is likely that halting consumer fraud was potentially a salient reward for a large segment of the neighborhood.

Costs of Participation

The experience of Du Pont with consumer fraud is illustrative of another major problem in securing participation in councils. Even after a council discovers what the salient rewards are, the people themselves do not necessarily wish to attain the reward through the council. One reason may be that the cost involved in working on a particular project may be too high. In a sensitive area such as fraud, public meetings and public discussions can be threatening to participants. People seldom like to expose themselves as having been gypped, and businessmen do not like to be publicly associated with fraud.

In seeking the support of the total community in dealing with problems, often obscured is the fact that certain groups or segments of the population are more vitally concerned than others with certain problems. In relation to these problems, these groups are the relevant community.[11] The relevant community cannot always be involved with the total community at formal council meetings. These public meetings may be useful only after long months of private discussions and informal meetings. In this vein Rein and Morris note "that it is often necessary to make decisions on important issues outside of the committee, not in order to undermine the democratic process, but to facilitate the process without destroying the committee through schism. . . . In this essentially ceremonious and harmony-creating capacity the committee system serves a useful purpose."[12]

Part of the reason for the overdependence on the formal committee meeting is a belief that if people come to committee meetings and are exposed to knowledge about the community, they will broaden their interests and develop into leaders or active participants. The fallacy lies in an inadequate appreciation of where involvement can take place. It cannot always take place in a council committee. For any of the reasons concerned with the costs of participation, an individual may only be able to be involved in his church group, or in private, or at the corner bar. The proof of this statement lies in the attendance figures of Du Pont. In the main people just did not come.

The consumer-fraud program illustrates another problem councils face in increasing participation. It was a project that presented salient rewards for one segment of the neighborhood, the low income, but salient costs to another, the businessmen. To the middle-class participants of Du Pont the project of consumer fraud was only of low saliency. The hope of finding highly salient projects to bring all segments of the neighborhood together is difficult to realize in non-crisis situations.

Recruitment

Hill had two basic reasons for wishing to recruit participants into the council. He wanted to change the attitudes and values of participants, and he wanted to effect important changes in the neighborhood, such as getting a new school or developing an urban renewal plan. The Du Pont experience points up that at times both types of changes can be accomplished with a rather small active group of participants. The council's history also reveals that many projects, such as consumer fraud, were dropped for lack of participation. In these cases Du Pont was unable to provide the rewards necessary to recruit the requisite participation.

One reason for the lack of rewards in participation was that the council did not provide all participants opportunities to use their resources. Those without middle-class organizational skills and resources were quickly frustrated. The activities of the Du Pont Health Committee illustrate this problem. The committee met nine times during the year, had a membership of ten and an average attendance of four, and accomplished almost nothing. The chairman was an extremely friendly, hardworking minister's wife, who was also a professionally trained social worker. The women on the committee actually attended out of loyalty to her. They were uninformed about health and, in the main, not verbal. Their resources were not of an intellectual or a technical nature. The group's initial project was to set up a first-aid course, but a teacher could not be secured from the Red Cross. The attempt dragged on over several months. Since it was obvious that the committee would need another project, several others were started: setting up sex education classes for teen-agers, compiling a health directory, organizing a blood bank, pressing for school health exams and a new general hospital, and supporting legislation on narcotics. None of these activities was successful, for each required more competence and skill than the members possessed.

As Schwartz has pointed out, the people who serve on committees must possess the requisites to achieve the committee's purposes.[13] Hill's hope seemed to be that the members of the health committee could develop or learn what was needed to achieve health goals through participation in the committee. However, this hope did not materialize because the committee died when the chairman left the neighborhood.

A technique that might have helped would have been to relate the activities of the committee to the resources available. Cloward and Piven note that the available resources dictate the structure of organizations as well as the tactics and programs these organizations can use in efforts of social change.[14] They imply that participation is related to providing opportunities for people to use the resources that they command. To do otherwise, in the hope that they can somehow learn to command new resources, would be self-defeating, for such an organization could not long remain alive.

Yet if goal attainment is viewed as primary, some goals will not be achievable with available resources, and the requisite resources must be recruited. In such cases non-selective recruitment can be self-defeating. Those who choose to participate may not have the needed resources. On the other hand, those who possess the needed resources may not wish to participate. In the area of politics and race relations, Du Pont was fortunate that it found a way out of this dilemma. Its answer was to get grass-roots participation in some areas—sports and the newspaper—and then pyramid these resources into influence in other areas—politics and race relations.

Of course, not every project can be achieved by using the available resources; nor can resources in most cases be pyramided easily. However, there is another option. Although Du Pont was continually urging projects on city departments, surprisingly, it never urged projects on its own member organizations. It only urged them to send representatives to the council. In the neighborhood there were two Roman Catholic sodalities and two women's Zionist organizations. These groups could have been asked to undertake particular health projects. The costs to individuals of working on a project in their own group would certainly be lower, the opportunities for maximizing rewards greater.

This tactic was not used because the council was considered a place where all groups could come and work together on common projects.

Probably, before this cooperation could occur, groups such as the Zionist and Catholic organizations would have to shift their orientation. Working on their own on a project suggested by Du Pont would be a start. Traditionally, councils have tried to connect themselves with local organizations by getting these organizations to send representatives to the council. An additional tactic could be to have the council send a representative to the group, in the person of the worker.

In addition, as noted earlier, one reason working- and lower-class people did not participate in the council was that opportunities were not provided for them to use or exchange the resources at their command. Providing them with opportunities to use such resources as technical competence in housing or knowledge of parliamentary procedure is not providing them with opportunities to participate. Small committee meetings, where verbal and technical competence are required, are poor structures in which to increase working- and lower-class participation. Since it is difficult to maintain all classes in one organization and since the working-class Puerto Rican and Chinese groups had no organizations of their own in the neighborhood, Du Pont could have attempted to foster organizations or projects geared to them.

Du Pont's attempt to recruit individual members of these groups was relatively unsuccessful. Even when some did join, they could not represent their ethnic groups in the sense of access to their resources, since the groups were not organized. All these individuals were able to give the council was their own personal resources. Had all Du Pont's members been so limited, the council would have been in difficulty. It was able to get along with a small group of active participants because some of these participants represented, in the sense of access to resources, large organizations and ethnic groups.[15]

Summary

Participation in Du Pont reflected its middle-class nature, its differential provision of rewards to certain ethnic groups, and its differential opportunities for the maximizing of rewards. The council was hampered in its attempts to increase participation because its recruitment appeals relied too heavily on its ability to discover salient projects or rewards for which all segments of the neighborhood could be involved within the confines of the council. Although these types of projects are valuable and participation at formal council meetings is necessary, there are other methods of recruitment that more fully take into account the costs of participation. For example, resources recruited for one purpose can be used for another. Men who would not invest their resources to improve race relations were willing to invest their resources in sports. Ultimately the resources invested in this manner were used to improve race relations. In addition, participation can be induced in already existing organizations as a prelude to council participation, or new organizations can be set up to ultimately supply the council with new resources, such as a Chinese language group or a Puerto Rican social club.

Councils whose recruitment is based on appeals to achieve specific goals, such as better housing, must consider the costs involved for participants in working toward the goal. To overcome these costs, the council's activities must be convertible to ideological, negotiable, and emotional rewards because participants occupy many statuses and will seek rewards for any or all of these statuses in their council activity. Participation is ultimately related to the opportunities for participation that a council affords. These opportunities must relate to the specific kinds of resources people have to exchange for the rewards a council offers. When a council provides opportunities only for the exchange of middle-class resources, it is actually engaging in selective recruitment of the middle class.

NOTES

1. For a discussion of various indices of social class, see Reinhard Bendix and Seymour Lipset, eds., *Class, Status and Power: A Reader in Social Stratification* (Glencoe, Ill.: Free Press, 1953). Participant data was derived from Appendix B, "Schedule for Interviewing Council Participants." Resident data was derived from *Codebook, Adult Survey,* vol. I (New York: Mobilization for Youth, 1962), p. 28.

2. *Codebook, Adult Survey,* vol. I, p. A-26, lists percentages for the HEED area: upper and middle class, 20.2%; lower and working class, 79.8%.

3. John M. Foskett, "The Influence of Social Participation on Community Programs and Activities," *Community Structure and Analysis,* ed. Marvin Sussman (New York: Thomas Y. Crowell, 1959), pp. 324–25.

4. Class rewards in this sense are not analogous to ethnic group rewards where members of an ethnic group desire rewards for their group, for example, Puerto Ricans want a meeting hall. Rewards as such do not redound to an individual because he is a member of a class in the Marxian sense and desires rewards for it, but merely redound to him because of certain attitudes, values, and skills he possesses that are determined by his social and economic position in society, that is, his class.

5. For a discussion of the factors that produced this attitude, see Edward C.

Banfield, *The Moral Basis of a Backward Society* (New York: Free Press, 1958).

6. A distinction is recognized between culturally determined rewards for ethnic groups—that is, Italians adhered to the Roman Catholic church—and situationally determined rewards for ethnic groups—that is, Italians derived emotional rewards because they felt the neighborhood was theirs.

7. Ward Hunt Goodenough, *Cooperation in Change* (New York: Russell Sage Foundation, 1963), p. 92.

8. Sills has noted the importance of emotional rewards to volunteers in the March of Dimes drive. He emphasizes the satisfactions related to task accomplishment, power over others, and the opportunity to be creative. David L. Sills, *The Volunteers* (Glencoe, Ill.: Free Press, 1957), pp. 151–58.

9. In a study of YMCA volunteers Arsenian and Blumberg note that people seldom mentioned commitment to YMCA principles as their reason for volunteering. They also note that people seldom came forward themselves; they had to be asked. Du Pont participants showed similar inclinations. As noted in table 12, ideological rewards were not the most significant for the majority of participants. See Seth Arsenian and Arthur Blumberg, "Volunteers in the Y.M.C.A.," *Association Forum*, XL (November-December 1959), 4–9.

10. See William C. Loring, Frank L. Sweetser, and Charles F. Ernst, *Community Organization for Citizen Participation in Urban Renewal* (Cambridge, Mass.: Cambridge Press, 1957), p. 6, or John Spencer, *Stress and Release in an Urban Estate* (London: Tavistock Publications, 1964), p. 25.

11. For a discussion of the relevant community, see Derek V. Roemer, "Focus in Programming for Delinquency Reduction," mimeographed (Washington, D.C.: National Institute of Mental Health, 1961).

12. Martin Rein and Robert Morris, "Goals, Structures and Strategies for Community Change," *Social Work Practice, 1962* (New York: Columbia University Press, 1962), p. 133.

13. Meyer Schwartz, "Our Voluntary Committee Life," *Journal of Jewish Communal Service*, XXXII (Spring 1956), 235–42. What Schwartz overlooks is that members of committees seldom possess all the needed requisites. Even if a committee begins work with members who have the necessary requisites, as the committee moves from one area of concern to another, members with different requisites are required. At times, the same committee may have advisory, pressure group, task, and educational functions. The pressure to get things done moves the committee into action before members with the needed requisites can be recruited. Failure is often the result.

14. Richard A. Cloward and Frances F. Piven, "Low-Income People and Political Process," mimeographed (New York: Mobilization for Youth, 1964).

15. For a discussion of the concept of representativeness, see Chauncey Alexander and Charles McCann, "Concept of Representativeness in Community Organization," *Social Work*, I (January 1956), 48–52.

9

Organizational Participation

Du Pont never made a clear choice between setting itself up as a mass organization of individuals or a representative organization of organizations. The decision to combine aspects of both was made by the executive committee for several reasons: first, most local organizations did not have the excess resources needed to maintain a council that was active in many areas of neighborhood life. Secondly, as table 18 indicates, large segments of the neighborhood were not rep-

TABLE 18
Representation of Residents in Local Organizations
(N=988)

Organizational Affiliation	Percentage of Residents
None	58.0%
One	28.0
Two	8.0
Three	3.5
Four	2.0
Five	.5

Source: Table was derived from *Codebook, Adult Survey*, vol. I (New York: Mobilization for Youth, 1962), p. 53.

resented in local organizations. Finally, conflicts among the local organizations made it unlikely that they would all support the council wholeheartedly.

Nevertheless, much of what Du Pont wanted to accomplish had to be done, of necessity, through other organizations, both of a member and a nonmember variety. The resources needed to build a new school rested with the board of education, those needed to organize a UNICEF carnival with the parents' associations, and the like. During the 1962–1963 program year, Du Pont interacted with fifty-eight different groups, indicating major organizational involvement. (See table 19.) In this chapter the council's involvement with its member organizations will be explored.[1]

TABLE 19

Organizations with Which Du Pont Interacted, 1962–1963

(N=58)

Nonmember Organizations	Number
State Agency	3
City department, agency	20
Public school	2
Political club	2
Citizens' improvement organization	4
Hospital, health center	3
Union	1
Recreation agency, association	4
Professional organization	2
Voluntary health, welfare organization	3
Foundation	1

Member Organizations	Number
Church	7
Political club	2
Parents' association	3
Settlement	1

Organizational Exchanges

In Du Pont, Jefferson House and the Protestant missions received the bulk of the rewards that the council offered. Through Du Pont their views on race relations were advanced, delinquency was defined in terms of lack of services, the doors of the political clubs were opened to their parishioners and members, and a new school was built at their demand. In 1963 HEED was attempting to organize another neighborhood council, SECA, twenty blocks north of Du Pont. In a year the settlement houses and missions in this council had done nothing more than write a constitution and clamor for more citizen participation.

Rewards to Organizations

Reid has noted, as have most community workers, that organizations do not necessarily cooperate simply because they share similar broad public goals.[2] Besides the neighborhood crisis, which tended to force cooperation, several other factors accounted for the commitment to the council of the Protestant churches and Jefferson House. Du Pont was geographically small, so the memberships of the agencies tended to overlap. It was common for teen-agers to go to several agencies. In other words, what went on in one had effects on the others. In addition, these agencies all felt that the Italian Catholic community was hostile to them, Finally, at least three of the agency directors were ideologically and professionally committed to neighborhood work. As noted earlier, each was able to advance his own career by his work in Du Pont.[3]

Costs to Organizations

Through the council the executives of Jefferson House and the Protestant missions were able to effect an exchange of resources, personnel, money, facilities, and contacts that made it possible to secure certain common goals that enhanced the organizational ends and personal ends of each. With the Roman Catholic churches and the regular political organizations, Du Pont was not able to enter into many exchanges. Besides the previously mentioned specific conflicts of interest that raised the costs of participation for these organizations, there were general costs that also affected their participation.

In our society there is a finite amount of time, money, skill, etc., available for voluntary activity. There exists a latent conflict among all organizations as to which is going to acquire the limited resources of people for participation. From this vantage point there is an inherent conflict between a council and neighborhood organizations. This discord is intensified by the possibility of a council's assuming the functions of local organizations.[4] If a council helps with housing problems, then a local political club can no longer exclusively perform this function and is weakened to the degree that this function had been important to its existence.[5] An individual may choose not to participate in a council or other voluntary organization without feeling adverse effects. However, if an organization does not participate, it can be affected adversely should one of its functions be weakened. Thus an organization must carefully consider its relation to another organization such as a council.

Rewards and Costs to the Council

An organization's participation has consequences for a council. One organization may be so antagonistic to another in a council that it refuses to join or participate. Another organization may be ideologically opposed to tactics such as picketing or parading, thereby limiting a council's actions.

There are more subtle consequences. Not only did there exist among the coalitional organizations in Du Pont a strong spirit of cooperation but also a strong commitment to better the neighborhood. However, there was a constraint on these organizations to define programs as being good for the neighborhood that, in reality, were often good for their organizations and not so good for the neighborhood or the council. A description of the 1963 summer program offered by the Du Pont Council illustrates this problem. The program included special events —trips to the beach or mountains, softball for young adults, outdoor movies, community dances, and a subsidized work program for teen-agers. Two facts stand out: the program was almost exclusively for teen-agers, and outside of the softball league, the program was attended almost exclusively by Negroes and Puerto Ricans. Staff members often sincerely deplored this fact; however, little effort was exerted toward dealing with the problem. Adult leaders of the white community were not contacted, nor were the white teen-age leaders.[6]

The summer program took the form that it did for several reasons. Primary was the reason that the summer planning committee was composed solely of representatives of the local youth-serving agencies. Secondly, the settlement house had received a substantial amount of money from its citywide affiliate, United Neighborhood Houses, on the basis that it would work with the council in providing a summer program for the neighborhood. This grant ensured a program since there was money for staff; if volunteers could not be found, then the staff could and did do the job. Although a strong case could be made that the neighborhood would have benefited more if some programs had been planned for adults or even for the white teen-agers, these programs did not materialize partly because of time and lack of resources.

Neighborhood people were invited, but did not come to planning meetings. In addition, without realizing it, as the summer came nearer, members of the committee shifted their thinking from what the neighborhood needed to what their own members needed.

The representatives of the coalitional organizations were anxious to meet the needs of people in the neighborhood, but they were influenced by their individual organization's needs for summer activities and programs. Du Pont suffered as an organization because of this influence. For example, it is doubtful if many people in the neighborhood knew that the summer program was under the sponsorship of the council. Besides, a program that was suitable to only one ethnic segment did not gain the council any support from other ethnic elements.

Major constraints on organizational representatives to a council are the time, money, goals, etc., of their home organization. Since, with the best of intentions, these representatives tend to define community needs and their own organization's needs as one and the same, they maximize rewards for their organization by their council activities. A major problem for a council like Du Pont, which is lead by an organizational coalition, is to ensure that the council's programs offer rewards to segments of the neighborhood not represented by the coalition. Otherwise the resources these segments possess cannot be recruited for the council. Since the Du Pont coalitional agencies did not have the resources to achieve many of the council's goals themselves, programs that tended to reward only coalitional organizations were self-defeating.

The Salient Reward

The relationships among organizations and the council can be expressed in a series of propositions:

1. Organizational interaction may be conceived as a form of exchange in which each organization attempts to maximize the rewards and lower the costs of their part of the exchange.
2. When there is a scarcity of needed organizational resources—time, money, personnel, commitment—local organizations are in actual or latent competition with one another for these resources and will thus be forced to develop tactics for dealing with one another.
3. Organizational perspectives on what constitutes community betterment will be determined in part by what the organization needs to survive and achieve its goals.

These propositions illustrate why organizational cooperation in a council is difficult to achieve. The costs of cooperation are too high for some, the rewards too low for others. The traditional community organization process has relied on building cooperative attitudes through participation with other organizations in council activities. The fact that most councils are short-lived suggests that these attitudes take considerable time to develop.[7] Initially, at least, a council would probably do better to rely on the rewards it has to offer organizations. Du Pont was able to develop quite an arsenal.

Linking Systems

In noncrisis situations it is unlikely that salient rewards will be generated by projects only tangentially related to the actual operating goals of organizations.[8] It may be assumed that an organization will be more apt to cooperate with the council if it can secure resources for the achievement of its goals while working on council goals. For example, the Little League and the UNICEF carnival achieved the goals of both the council and its organizations. As the SECA experience illustrates, bringing all local organizations together around a table does not guarantee that they will arrive at projects that will offer their organizations salient rewards. The SECA organizations settled on such projects as getting better bus service, improving East End Park, improving day-care facilities, and promoting a job rally. None of these were related to the real goals of these organizations. Since none could be achieved easily, the organizations began to lose interest quickly. The norm that an organization should be community-minded simply was not sufficient to sustain participation in the face of mounting costs.

To secure organizational participation, a staff worker should be concerned with the development of programs directly related to the real goals of organizations.[9] However, it is not necessary for all organizations to participate for the same reason. A case in point is the activities of the Harold Street Strip subcommittee. Ostensibly this subcommittee was set up to improve the housing on Harold Street. It was made up of two priests, the leader of the reform Democratic club, a social worker from a Harold Street settlement house outside of the Du Pont area, and the cochairmen of the Du Pont Housing Committee.

Father D., an Anglican priest, was interested in Harold Street because his church was situated on the worst part of it. The condition of the housing and the street affected the image of his church. Monsignor Longue was building a new parochial school nearby. He was interested in what happened to housing because he was trying to plan the size of his new school. Mr. Peter, the leader of the reform club, wanted to gain exposure in the neighborhood. During the fall primary his campaign literature claimed that his club had secured the city's promise to set up an area services project to improve Harold Street housing.

All these men may sincerely have wanted to improve the life of the people on Harold Street. Yet behind their perseverance was also the fact that the project was related to a vital resource that they needed to attain the real goals of their individual organizations. Again it can be seen that a council is able to increase organizational participation by relating its projects directly to the resources that organizations need to pursue their real goals.

Developing Exchanges

It is unlikely that a council would long survive if it had to depend exclusively on relating all its projects to the vital resources needed by organizations. All projects cannot be so related. A more effective tactic is for a council to try to develop over a period of time a basis of exchange with organizations. Du Pont always publicly urged the political clubs to support the council's activities based on appeals to the general welfare. Yet its attempt was never really successful until a base of exchange with the clubs had been built.

These exchanges were often the result of the latent functions of programs.[10] The newspaper provided the council with the resource to praise or criticize, promote or oppose. The Town Hall meeting gave it prestige and an aura of potential power. The Little League parade gave the council visibility. All these resources were also useful to politicians.

Imposition of Costs

An additional element in the Du Pont experience adds significantly to practice knowledge about participation. There are occasions when rewards alone will not suffice. Conflicts of interests and values negate the effects of the rewards that a council can offer. In such cases, when people or organizations do not wish to accept the rewards that a council offers because the costs are too high, the council must be able to raise the costs of nonparticipation to such a degree that they outweigh the costs of participation. For example, in the sports committee one Italian church engaged in a concerted campaign to get the committee to secede from the council. In part it was prevented from achieving this end or from dropping out itself because of a fear of losing prestige by being labeled as prejudiced or the cause of the Little League's breaking up.

Likewise, the imposition of costs for nonparticipation played a significant part in the success of the Harold Street Strip subcommittee's work. Note the following:

Father [D.] reported that the group was following up on the institutions to see that they sent telegrams and letters to the mayor and the head of the Planning Commission. Mr. [S.] said that he was very appreciative of the Democratic boss in the area sending a telegram. There was some joking about the fact that the politicians seemed to be responding faster than the social agency heads.[11]

Reverend [D.] was not present. The worker reported on the meeting with Mr. Marlin of the Housing and Redevelopment Board. He noted that Mr. Marlin had been very encouraging. He said that the council's campaign to influence the city to award it an Area Services Project was classic and was one that could be studied by every other citizen's group.[12]

The politicians did respond more quickly than the social workers. Although the Count had never before concerned himself with housing, with a primary fight in the offing he could not afford to let the reform leader gain an advantage.

Even Du Pont's limited ability to impose costs for nonparticipation played a significant part in securing the support of local organizations. The imposition of these costs rests on a council's ability to gain control over a resource that an organization views as vital for its existence. With the political club it was votes, with the church prestige.

Lowering Costs

Another factor that affects organizational participation in councils is that some organizations are too weak to supply resources to a council. For example, at a meeting of the Johnson Square Council, another of the HEED councils, the following incident occurred: at the end of the first program meeting of the year, an elderly lady from a Jewish women's organization asked what her group could do for the council. She was assured by the chairman that she would be contacted. Clearly the intention was to recruit members from her group to the council. Conceivably, participation in meetings and on council projects might be impossible for such an organization because its resources might be adequate only for maintaining itself. Before asking an organization for resources such as members, a council should know something about that organization's strength. Instead of asking weak organizations to provide resources, it could ask them to sponsor under their own aegis projects that might help the neighborhood as well as the group itself.[13]

Individual and Organizational Participation

Du Pont was more an organization of organizations than a mass citizens' group. For instance, in the Harold Street Strip subcommittee there were no residents of Harold Street. No great effort was made to recruit them because they actually were not needed. As noted, the members of the committee had vital stakes in the street. They did not feel it necessary to go through the arduous process of getting local residents on the committee because they felt that they could mobilize the political power to obtain the area services project. However, it was not until 1965 that the city actually opened an area services project on Harold Street. There is, of course, no assurance that a committee of residents would have had more immediate results, but they probably would have used different techniques during 1964 when the project was stalled. The subcommittee translated its concern during the months of inaction into phone calls and a series of letters from Hill to city officials.

A significant fact is pointed out by the workings of the Harold Street subcommittee and the summer planning committee: when projects present salient rewards for organizations, these organizations will commit their resources to these projects. In doing this, they tend not to attempt to recruit the resources of individual citizens since such efforts are time-consuming and costly. Even if they achieve their goals, the implication is that individual citizens are not needed.

One council project and the way it is carried out will have effects on others. When the council considers projects that are not of high saliency to organizations, such as consumer fraud, then individual citizens are needed. Yet at these times citizens may not come forward due to the image the council has projected. Had the Harold Street Strip project been carried out with residents of the street, it is likely, at the least, that the consumer-fraud project would not have been dropped so abruptly. One of the sports committee members stated the problem succinctly: "Paid staff of agencies and volunteers can't be on the same committee."

To maintain a balance between individual and organizational participation, Du Pont would have had to control, at least in part, the makeup of the committees and the actions these committees took. This control is difficult to impose because committees tend to view their work narrowly and do not ordinarily take into account the organizational ramifications.[14] If a balance between organizational and individual participation is required in a council, then maintaining the balance is an important area of concern for a staff worker. In other than the summer planning committee, Du Pont was fortunate in having members who were not directly affiliated with the coalition organizations.

Summary

Few neighborhood organizations as a matter of daily routine allocate a share of their resources to projects for neighborhood betterment. Therefore, such improvement is not an operating goal of most organizations. In seeking to impose a degree of control on local organizations, councils must seek a reallocation of organizational resources. There may be slack resources available in some organizations for investing in community-betterment projects tangential to their real or operating goals. Yet, the importance of attaining their operating goals will necessarily limit most organizations' participation.

Du Pont was successful in maintaining its coalition because the executives of three of the coalition organizations made community improvement a prime operating goal of their organizations. Merely providing knowledge about community needs and an opportunity for organizations to discuss them were not enough to ensure the participation of other organizations. When Du Pont was successful in securing the participation of noncoalition agencies, it did so mainly by offering exchanges that aided them in the pursuit of their operating goals.

Community control cannot be achieved by a council solely through appeals geared to social values or rational ends such as the more effective provision of services. There are overt and latent conflicts among local organizations. Tactics such as linking systems, pyramiding resources to build exchanges, and imposing costs for nonparticipation must be utilized.

NOTES

1. Whereas individual local residents had merely to come to meetings to be considered a member, local organizations had to pay a $25 membership fee.
2. William Reid, "Interagency Co-ordination in Delinquency Prevention and Control," *Social Service Review*, XXXVIII (December 1964), 419.

3. Though the neighborhood situation was different in 1966 than it was in 1956, the departure of these men from the neighborhood was in all cases followed by a lessened commitment to Du Pont of their agencies. It would seem that the orientation of their personal career was an important factor in maintaining the coalition.

4. Ross's view of council functioning is limited. He notes that a council is only as strong as its constituent member organizations. Yet Du Pont was strong to the degree that it was able to weaken some of its constituent organizations. See Murray G. Ross, *Community Organization* (New York: Harper and Bros., 1955), pp. 184–85.

5. There are thus rewards and costs available in a council that go to the maintenance and the enhancement of organizations rather than solely to the needs of individuals. To understand council functioning, it is important to understand this distinction.

6. It must be pointed out that when the program was instituted in 1956–1957, some white adults and teen-agers did participate. Also some programs were geared to adults. However, by 1962–1963 the participation composition had changed.

7. The intent is not to deny the utility of trying to develop norms of cooperation, but to point out that appeals to such cannot be exclusively relied on to increase participation. In addition, it may be speculated that in situations where community organizers report success in gaining organizational cooperation, further analysis would show that a good deal of exchange—related and unrelated to the project at hand—actually went on.

8. A real operating goal is defined as one toward which an agency regularly allocates a major share of its resources. One way to gauge the actual goals of an organization is to check to what ends its resources are allocated. An agency's public espousal of goals for neighborhood betterment does not necessarily mean that such goals are operative in the agency.

9. For a discussion of the concept of "systemic linkage," see Charles P. Loomis, "Toward a Theory of Systemic Social Change," *Interprofessional Training Goals for Technical Assistance Personnel Abroad* (New York: Council on Social Work Education, 1959).

10. In addition to the latent functions of a council's programs, the latent functions that a council itself performs as an entity are often that which account for a large part of the council's ability to secure participation. Vidich and Bensman present evidence of a "community club" that actually was the innovating organization for change in a community. This club was able to innovate because it was expedient for the political party in power to use the club to try out new projects, thereby lessening the chance for the opposition party to make political capital out of mistakes and errors. See Arthur J. Vidich and Joseph Bensman, *Small Town in Mass Society* (Princeton, N.J.: Princeton University Press, 1958), p. 132.

Festinger describes a council that was the first formal organization in a new neighborhood. It was able to retain considerable vitality as an organization for improvement because through council activities people first met others and formed lasting friendships. These friendships served to reinforce loyalty to the council and thus enhanced its stability and effectiveness. See Leon Festinger, Stanley Schachter, Kurt Bach, *Social Pressures in Informal Groups* (Stanford:

Stanford University Press, 1950), pp. 68–71.

For a general discussion of the latent functions of voluntary organizations, see Arnold Rose, *Theory and Method in the Social Sciences* (Minneapolis: University of Minnesota Press, 1954), pp. 50–51, 68–71. John R. Seeley et al. in *Community Chest: A Case Study in Philanthropy* (Toronto: University of Toronto Press, 1957) analyze community chests from the vantage point of latent functions.

11. Du Pont Executive Committee field notes, March 13, 1963.

12. Du Pont Housing Committee field notes, April 18, 1963.

13. In order to overcome the costs of participation to individuals, a useful tactic is to let organizations sponsor council projects so that while their members are working on such projects, they can continue to accrue the rewards they usually get from participation in the organization (maximization of rewards). Likewise, from an organizational point of view, there is value in letting weak organizations sponsor council projects. Both from an individual and organizational standpoint these are compelling reasons for a council to refrain from constantly recruiting everyone into its formal committees.

14. Selznick cogently states that "it is generally true that where the class, family, sectional, or ethnic origins of personnel are uncontrolled, unanticipated consequences for decision making may ensue." See Phillip Selznick, *The Organizational Weapon: A Study of Bolshevik Strategy and Tactics* (New York: McGraw-Hill, 1952), p. 60.

10

Goal Attainment

Du Pont was successful in achieving a number of its goals related to local institutions, religious, political, and educational. As noted in table 20, it also had some success in affecting the attitudes and ideas of its participants.

TABLE 20
What Members Learned Through Participation
(N=75)

Response	Percentage of Members
Learned about the neighborhood and its problems	28%
Learned that things can be accomplished by cooperating	27
Learned what to do to solve neighborhood problems	24
Learned to respect other groups	17
Learned little or nothing	17
Learned other miscellaneous things	7

NOTE: See Appendix B, "Schedule for Interviewing Council Participants." Total adds to more than 100% due to multiple coding.

These two target areas—the attitudes and values of council participants and the functioning of neighborhood institutions—reflect an important difference in approach within the field of community organization. The former is regarded as the major target of the *process* orientation; the techniques associated with this orientation are to an extent therapeutic in their conception. They focus on individual change and heightened social consciousness. The *institutional* view, on the other hand, directs itself toward changing social institutions through quasi-political strategies based on social organization.[1]

The Lack of *Process* in Du Pont

Process in its ideal form was not carried out in Du Pont. What is revealed through observation of Du Pont's activities is that the attitudes and values of participants may be changed, to a limited degree through participation, even when the traditional process orientation is not followed.

The essential element of process—a sequential problem-solving procedure geared to the development of collaborative attitudes—is that the worker uses his *method* to make the process conscious, deliberative, and understood.[2] There are a number of reasons why the ideal process did not occur in Du Pont. One reason is that the vast majority of members did not view the council as an educational organization or one that developed leadership skills. (See table 21.) Rewards came from getting things done. Spencer and his colleagues have concluded from their research of councils in "new towns" in England that the process of "education through involvement" can occur only when those involved in the process are thoroughly committed to learning as their major reason for being in the council. Otherwise, confusion and frustration

TABLE 21
What Should the Council Do?
(N=83)

Response	Percentage of Members
Solve problems in various areas	83%
Educate citizens, develop leaders	17
Promote neighborliness	18
Promote participation for all groups	15
Others	1

NOTE: See Appendix B, "Schedule for Interviewing Council Participants." Totals add to more than 100% due to multiple coding.

over lack of action will result.[3] Since internal pressure to take action in committees is often considerable, it is likely that many educational opportunities will be missed.[4]

Many such opportunities were missed in Du Pont. Not only were the members not primarily concerned with understanding the process but the worker was not primarily concerned with teaching them. Hill's efforts and interests lay in the area of goal attainment. Numerous situations occurred in which he might have generalized problems and led discussions that could have given members new insights and ideas. Two such opportunities occurred in the education and executive committee meetings:

At this meeting there was a constant reference to the school bureaucracy. The school principals would not give information and the school superintendent did not like a certain program. The problems were never considered in any of their broader dimensions, such as the controls on people in a bureaucracy, methods of securing responsiveness, etc. They were discussed in very narrow terms such as the personality and status needs of the superintendent.[5]

The problem of financing kept coming up. Mr. [M.] mentioned that at one time they used to get money from the parents of the children who played in the Little League. There were other mentions of the budget to be presented to HEED, and whether organizations had paid their dues. These things were simply mentioned and dropped.[6]

The expertise of a few members of Du Pont also made it somewhat unlikely that Hill would make the process conscious, deliberative, and understood. Although these members could be relied upon to give freely of their knowledge and talent, they seldom passed on this knowledge. They did not view themselves as teachers, and their presence negated the need for others really to become involved in the process. This problem is pointed out by the following:

One of the problems of the Council is illustrated by the fact that with Reverend [O.'s] leaving the neighborhood no one can really replace him as editor of the *News*. No one has learned the skills although the newspaper has been running for seven years and many people have been active during the whole period.[7]

The presence of such experts also reinforced control by an elite in Du Pont.[8] The executive committee actually ran the council. General membership meetings were used to drum up interest and participation in programs rather than to create a setting for carrying through process. Members of the executive committee seldom attended general meetings. They knew that if anything of substance occurred it would ultimately reach the executive committee. Oligarchy, then, is antithetical to process.

Ross suggests that if process is to take place, the community organization "must be . . . content to deal only with those problems about which there is or can be unanimous, or almost unanimous agreement."[9] The coalition that ran Du Pont was not interested in dealing only with issues for which there was neighborhood consensus. Yet it did not approach sensitive issues like racial segregation in the political clubs through open and full discussion. A problem on which consensus could not be achieved—one that might split the council—was generally handled informally by the leaders of the coalition. The consequence was suppression of full-membership participation and enhancement of control by an oligarchy.

A final reason that process did not occur in Du Pont was that the need of the council to survive was a continuing factor to be dealt with. Although the women on the health committee might have learned a good deal through participation, there was no way to sustain the committee long enough for that to happen. To keep committees alive, projects were often instituted without full discussion and without any real study of the neighborhood. Discussions were held not so much to inform people about problems but to interest them in participating. The emphasis on maintaining participation precluded following the process.

Thus it is clear that process can take place only under extremely specialized situations: members have to define their role as something akin to a student or a client; tendencies toward oligarchy must be restrained; projects must be those for which there is consensus and about which there can be full discussion; and sufficient resources and interest must be available so that needs for survival do not become pre-eminent. Du Pont did not provide these requisites for process.

Exchanges and Planning for Goal Attainment

Du Pont was geared to attaining specific goals in the neighborhood. In its efforts the council encountered many problems, which may be seen in the context of member-organization exchanges. One of these problems related to goal selection.

Goal Selection

Du Pont was often forced to choose among many worthwhile projects. As the range of ratings in table 22 illustrates, members did not share common standards for assigning priority.[10] Each person assigned priority on the basis of what he felt was good for the neighborhood and the council. A precise and strategic selection of council projects, therefore, cannot be based on a poll of members' attitudes.

TABLE 22

Active Members' Assignment of Priority to Projects
(N=22)

Project	Mean Rank	Standard Deviation	Range of Ratings
Curbing delinquency	3.9	1.8	3.6
Providing better employment opportunities	3.5	1.9	3.8
Studying honesty of storekeepers	9.0	1.9	3.8
Improving health facilities	6.0	2.0	4.0
Organizing social functions	8.7	2.4	4.8
Dealing with interracial relations	3.1	2.4	4.8
Improving schools	3.3	2.4	4.8
Handling tenant-landlord problems	5.0	2.4	4.8
Creating better credit facilities	7.7	2.8	5.6
Offering family-living courses	6.2	2.8	5.6
Providing more recreational facilities	5.2	4.6	9.2

NOTE: See Appendix B, "Schedule for Interviewing Council Participants."
Each project was assigned a priority rating from 1 to 11 by each active participant. Thus on an 11-point scale a range of 3 or less was selected as a reasonable spread for an index of consensus. The range of ratings on each project exceeds this limit.

In addition, although some projects may be good for the neighborhood, they may not necessarily be good for the council. For example, the adult-education specialist of the board of education wanted Du Pont to organize adult-education classes; the local liaison with the board of health wanted the council to participate in various health campaigns; the civil rights groups, in their programs. Although these projects all were designed to improve the neighborhood, they also served to promote and preserve the organizations sponsoring them and helped these groups to compete with the council for resources.

As an aid for selecting projects, a classification of project goals can be derived based on where exchanges will have to be made to get the resources necessary for project completion. It is thus possible to distinguish the following: contract-out goals, where one large organization or department contains all the resources and attains the goal for the council; cooperative goals, where several organizations pool these resources under the aegis of the council; and do-it-yourself goals, where the council controls all the necessary resources. This classification can help in gauging the effects of projects on a council.

As table 23 illustrates, Du Pont maintained a balance among these three types of goals. Relying exclusively on any one type would present risks to a council. For example, there are many reasons, not apparent at the local level, why services cannot immediately be contracted for with city agencies. Often there are not enough resources to provide for every neighborhood's needs. In addition, only a few participants receive the rewards involved in the actual negotiating with the city. As time goes on and few results are attained, the costs mount for others not so immediately involved. It can be surmised that many councils flounder because they choose only the kind of goals where other organizations contain the resources and must produce the service. Du Pont

TABLE 23

Successes and Failures of 1962–1963 Projects

	Project		
Type of Goal	Successfully Completed	Still in Process	Failed to Complete
Contract-out	Replacement of PS 4 Harold Street Strip Police protection	Replacement of JH 13 Housing Du Pont urban renewal Ditch and Boundary Streets Civic center plan	Jones Softball Field Garibaldi Park renewal Home nursing course School health exams
Cooperative	UNICEF carnival Brotherhood Week Summer program Little League		Blood bank
Do-it-yourself	Homework helper Health questionnaire Newspaper Office opening Going-away dinner	Civil rights	Health directory Sex-education program Canister campaign Consumer fraud

took four to five years to achieve the urban renewal plan and the new school. Without its other types of goals and the rewards derived from them, the council would not have survived.

Goals that require coordination among various organizations are difficult to achieve because they necessarily call for some loss of organizational autonomy, function, etc. Thus some organizations judge coordinated objectives as too costly. Whereas the church missions and Jefferson House produced a summer program through Du Pont, the same kind of agencies were not willing to work jointly elsewhere in HEED. As noted earlier, project coordination is difficult to bring about in non-crisis situations unless the project offers organizations resources for use in other systems in which they operate.

Perhaps the most typical goal that councils choose is the do-it-yourself type. Generally a service is produced through these projects. Although they provide major rewards for task accomplishment, most often these projects require great inputs of time, money, skill, etc. which councils generally have in limited supply. There is a danger that a council may exhaust itself in pursuing these projects, especially when the projects do not have an immediate payoff in rewards or are of such short duration and limited effect that participants become demoralized —as would be the case with a never-used community-needs survey or a street cleanup that takes two weeks to organize but only two days to return to its former state. Do-it-yourself projects seem best advised when they are of a permanent nature and emotional rewards are regularly available, such as in the newspaper committee or in cases when participants have an ideological commitment to the project.

Part of Du Pont's success was due to its ability to maintain a balance among the three types of project goals. This mixture provided a supply of long-term and short-term rewards, as well as an opportunity for developing rewards in one type useful for exchange in another type.[10] For example, the do-it-yourself newspaper was useful in gaining the cooperation of the politicians, who were useful in getting the city to contract out for the area services project. This combination of project goals was not the result of a conscious plan in the council, but emerged over the years as the group looked for new projects to undertake, while holding on to the old bulwarks, such as the Little League and the newspaper.

The selection of projects is a crucial decision for councils. The analysis of the exchanges inherent in a project will not provide a definitive answer as to whether a project should be undertaken. There are questions to be answered about the extent of knowledge available on certain social problems, about timing and sanction of the "right to plan" and take action, and whether solutions to some problems are available at the local level. There are also vital decisions to be made about the possibility of developing the capacity to achieve certain goals.[11] Nevertheless, the analysis of exchanges can be of considerable help.

Goal Relationships

The broad goals that councils have can rarely be achieved by any one project. A new school, for instance, would likely be part of a series of projects that a council would sponsor to change educational patterns in a neighborhood. Therefore, each project should be planned so that it can enhance future projects.

Some of the health committee's difficulty lay in its inability to relate its projects in such a way as to be able to develop its limited resources to the point where it could significantly affect local health conditions. Its inability to plan on bases other than the health value of specific projects was illustrated at a general meeting concerned with local health needs:

Mr. [S.] tried to press Dr. Lear into specifying just what it is that local groups can do other than public education, and advising professionals on the appropriate place for facilities and the needs of the community. Dr. Lear suggested citizens should take the lead in getting the professionals together.[12]

In essence, it was suggested that in Du Pont the pivotal target group for improving health conditions was not the citizens, not the department of health, not the department of hospitals, but individual medical practitioners in the neighborhood. This idea of recruiting the resources of local doctors was not taken up. Hill and council members were concerned with what a local group of citizens could do in the area of health. The response of Du Pont members to Dr. Lear's suggestion was that "the doctors are too busy and overworked as is." No doubt they were, but this situation might have been exploited by the council.

Instead of going off in six directions at once, the health committee could have offered to help doctors with certain recurrent yet routine problems that they had to contend with: the aged invalid who needed someone to get her medicine from the drugstore; the non-English-speaking mother who did not understand the proper use of medicine; the family with so many problems it was ready to fall apart. In a sense the health committee could have been the doctors' private social agency. Exchanges entered into in such a relationship could have formed the basis of a health committee made up of citizens, doctors, and nurses. In addition, such doctor-helper activities could have aided in race relations because they would have provided opportunities for adults of different races to work together for one another. The committee would have also provided meaningful activities for the less verbal, increased the level of awareness about the neighborhood, and most importantly, offered the council an opportunity to use the resources of the local physicians in negotiations with the local hospital administrator, the department of health, etc.

Goal Displacement

Another set of factors that councils must consider in planning projects relates to the time required to carry them out and the resources needed. If these factors are not considered, a project will either fail or goal displacement will occur. For example, the health committee had insufficient skill to put out a health directory, got bogged down in trying to contract out for a home-nursing course, and was not able to muster the influence to get the schools to cooperate in giving health examinations. The failure of the committee was not apparent until the end of the year—and even then not to most members because projects were to be carried over to the next year.

Members of the health committee received emotional rewards that compensated for their lack of goal achievement. They enjoyed the sociability; the once-a-month morning meeting was a pleasant coffee klatch. The committee was able to survive for as long as it did because of the emergence of these rewards, which somewhat deflected the committee from its goal or at least prevented it from assessing what it had really accomplished.

In business organizations there are emergent rewards of status, sociability, fraternity, and the like. However, when the primary, tangible reward of money sinks below a certain level, the organization is forced to reappraise its situation. In contrast a council can often exist for longer periods on emergent rewards unrelated to the attainment of its goals. Although these rewards may be functional for participants and for the stability of a council, in terms of the goals of a committee or its council, they may defeat its purposes and ultimately change the objectives of the organization. As noted, the health committees' goals were selected because they seemed worthwhile and because people seemed interested in working on them. Had Hill more fully considered how long it would take to accomplish some of these goals and what kinds of resources were available, he might have chosen short-term projects, which could have been accomplished with the resources at hand. Then, through these projects additional resources might have been procured to carry on long-term projects.

Exchanges and the Tactics of Goal Attainment

Much of the criticism of neighborhood councils is based on the assumption that in seeking to involve the total neighborhood, they perforce tend toward consensus. The projects that councils choose, and the tactics that they use to carry them out, will, therefore, reflect this consensus rather than the conflicts that exist in an area.[13] From this point of view, a council could be expected to press for better police protection rather than raise the issue of police brutality, or publicize a polio campaign rather than protest poor medical treatment given to welfare recipients. A dramatic illustration of this tendency occurred at a meeting of SECA, one of the HEED councils. To announce the opening of a housing clinic, the housing chairman prepared a leaflet entitled "Fight the Landlord." The chairman of SECA vigorously protested this tactic, saying that it was not fair to castigate all the landlords. The title of the leaflet was subsequently changed to "Do Something About Your Housing Problems."

Yet Du Pont's activities already noted indicate that the council took a range of actions, many consensual, some highly controversial. Over the years the council became involved in and, at times, won ethnic battles. It supported a school boycott in 1964, an unapproachable activity in 1958. Local institutions were made considerably more responsive to Negro and Puerto Rican needs.

Management of Conflict

The leadership of Du Pont was keenly aware of the limts on its ability to enter into conflict. The costs of some controversial projects were so high that they threatened the existence of the council. The insurgent political clubs were formed outside of the council to help to alleviate this threat. Overall council strategy was to increase the area in which it could engage in conflict.[14] To a certain extent the council's public espousal of neighborhood consensus and cooperation as values enabled the council to set itself up as the conscience or voice of the neighborhood. Thus the council had some license for promoting conflict—as it did when it chastised the politicians in the *Du Pont News*.

Essentially the council used conflict to generate exchanges. In striving for a replacement for PS 4, the *Du Pont News* fomented conflict; and just when the neighborhood was ready for a mass protest or confrontation, it cooled out the neighborhood, thereby gaining a valuable resource to exchange with the local school personnel. In general the council's tactic was to avoid confrontations and manage conflict in ways that enhanced its ability to enter into exchanges that would strengthen its position in the conflict. The first and most obvious use to which racial conflict was put was that it was the raison d'être of the council's formation as well as of the Little League's origin. Once the League was formed, rules, regulations, and appeals to sportsmanship contained conflict on the playing field and the sports committee.

Although it might be argued that an organization composed solely of Negroes, Puerto Ricans, and their allies might have engaged more directly in issues of conflict and perhaps might have had more effect, Du Pont achieved a great deal in the area of race relations through the tactic of maintaining or guiding conflict. The council was able to increase its ability to engage in conflict over the years as it solidified its position in the neighborhood and did not have to fear secession of some groups.

Of course, had the Italian organizations fully participated in the affairs of the council, they could have lessened Du Pont's leverage in managing conflict by vetoing or stalling what they opposed.[15] Thus Du Pont's ability to engage in conflict was related in part to the lack of a concerted and organized opposition. It may be speculated that only when such conditions exist can a neighborhood council made up of all local organizations and groups effectively engage in conflict. Such a council would, however, have to be skilled in keeping an organized opposition from developing.

Leadership

The ability of Du Pont's leadership was a major factor in its success. As table 24 illustrates, participants related the qualities for successful leadership to a set of general organizational skills and personal traits, rather than expertise in solving neighborhood problems or possession of concrete resources. However, looking at Du Pont from the point of view of how it created exchanges to achieve its goals, the ability to lead was based on much more than a set of rational skills and personality traits. To achieve many of its goals in the neighborhood, the leadership had to possess such requisites as influence over people and groups, control of money and facilities, and membership in particular ethnic groups. Dennis, as noted, has commented that of the councils he observed in England, those which survived were able to replace their leadership when it was no longer adequate to the tasks required of it.[16] According to his viewpoint, leadership must either have access to or possess the requisites needed by an organization to achieve its goals and survive.

TABLE 24

Participants' Perception of an Ideal Chairman
(N=67)

Response	Percentage of Participants
Personality and character traits	61%
General organizational skills	61
Knowledge and concern about neighborhood	45
Expertise in solving neighborhood problems	12
Control over concrete resources	12
Others	1

NOTE: See Appendix B, "Schedule for Interviewing Council Participants." General organizational skills refer to the ability to run meetings, present the Council's point of view, adjudicate differences, etc. Control over concrete resources refers to having contacts, possessing money, access to facilities, etc. Table adds to more than 100% due to multiple coding.

The leaders of Du Pont's coalition talked about leadership in terms of resources. For example, at a nominating committee meeting, the chairman said, "I don't think the community is ready for a Negro chairman." For achieving the council's goals in the area of racial integration, a Negro chairman was viewed as much less useful than an Italian chairman. A less sophisticated group might simply have considered any bright, interested person without regard to his potential effect on specific council goals.

Yet this practical sophistication never altered the manifest belief that leadership is simply a matter of training and the council should act as such a training ground.[17] The director of Jefferson House felt that a council could be successful in any neighborhood and that he as a staff worker could organize such a council if given the opportunity. He failed to see the difference between his position in Du Pont—where he commanded a staff of twenty, possessed facilities large enough to accommodate ten councils, and had access to considerable amounts of money and influence—and his position in "X" neighborhood as a person trying to organize a council in which he commanded nothing but himself.

Although the directors of the coalition agencies admitted that they were the leaders of Du Pont, they attributed this leadership chiefly to their executive and administrative capacities. These capacities did play a great part; however, from an exchange point of view the command of other vital resources that the council needed—such as access to agency facilities and staff—was an equally important determinant of leadership position. Members of the coalition thought that if new leaders could be developed, they themselves could become less active. They hoped that the council could get along without them. However, for this to have occurred, the council would have had to develop a new source of resources. Without this source, formal offices could be filled by other people who possessed rational leadership skills, but few decisions could be made without a commitment of the coalition's resources. Thus the coalition de facto would still be in control. To divest itself of leadership in the council, the coalition would have had to develop these sources or have trained its replacements to develop them.

Developing Resources

Du Pont needed vital resources that no amount of training or experience would help a person to gain. A chairman cannot be trained to be an Italian; nor can he be trained to have access to agency facilities. Yet within these limits there are ways of learning how to gain vital resources.

The primary insight that an exchange concept affords in relation to goal attainment, whether the goal be better schools, housing, or race relations, is that resources do not always have to be directly recruited for the project at hand; nor do they have to be immediately available to complete the project successfully. A call does not have to go out immediately for people to attend a meeting for a new school. A more successful strategy is likely to be one that appraises the kinds of resources a council will need to attain the goal beforehand and then plans out a potential series of exchanges that the council will have to enter into to get these needed resources.

Instead of dropping a project when required resources are not immediately available through usual council procedures, a council's leadership has other options. It can attempt to recruit for another project resources that could be pyramided for use in the first. Resources pyramided in this way played a vital part in the attainment of many of Du Pont's goals: newspaper resources were used for urban renewal, Little League resources for politics, UNICEF carnival resources for school construction. The leadership can attain a goal by setting up new organizations in which the costs of investing the needed resources would be lower than in the council. Or it can get already existing organizations to undertake the project. It can carry out a project in such a way as to provide rewards to individuals and organizations in systems they participate in other than those related to the project, for example, the supplying of rewards to the Catholic church by the Little League. It can also attempt to control a needed resource, such as threatening the loss of prestige to impose costs for nonparticipation.

In deciding on appropriate tactics, it is important for a council to appraise the range of procedures open to it: mass meetings, parades, committee meetings, forums, delegations, surveys, etc. An exchange concept provides such a method of appraisal. What rewards are inherently related to the procedure? what costs? Will those who must carry out the procedure find it rewarding? Does the procedure enhance the council's ability to offer rewards in exchange for needed resources? A council must be able to adapt procedures to the resources available or select procedures suited to recruiting the needed resources.

Most of the exchanges that Du Pont entered into occurred by chance or seemed obvious under the circumstances. For instance, the Catholic churches would only participate if they controlled their boys; the old newspaper of the Jones and the T.V. Housing Projects happened to be folding; the Town Hall meeting was held more out of desperation than design. The other HEED councils, SECA, Good Samaritan, and Johnson Square, were in the main weak and ineffectual. The HEED workers were not able to translate the Du Pont experience into terms useful for the other councils.

The Good Samaritan Council covered an area similar to Du Pont and adjacent to it. This council floundered for three years trying to get people to join its committees. The same conflicts between whites and Negroes and between the middle class and the lower class existed here. Had the organizational problems been conceptualized in terms of resources and rewards, then the possibilities of working separately with only one or all of the conflicting groups or the possibility of providing rewards that could bridge the conflict would have come to the fore.

Summary

A council must be able to devise a plan of action to attain its goals. It must know where problems can be solved and who can solve them. Seldom will the needed resources be readily available. The first task in relation to any project goal is to locate from which groups, organizations, and individuals the required resources can be secured. The second is to develop a plan to get these resources. If those who possess the resources do not wish to invest them in the project, then the council must develop its capacity to induce this investment.

In Du Pont resources recruited for one project produced rewards that were used to recruit resources for a second. Some problems were solved outside of the council in other organizations.

A council that is primarily interested in achieving control over a community and its institutions will be constrained to develop tactics and strategies that cannot always be publicly pronounced. To this extent democratic procedures in a council will be altered, and control, if imposed, will actually be vested in a few decision makers.

NOTES

1. Recent research findings suggest the dysfunctions of dichotomizing these approaches and support the view that efforts aimed solely at changing attitudes will not be effective in achieving this change. Festinger sums up this research by noting: "It is my present contention that in order to produce a stable behavior change following opinion change, an environmental change must also be produced which, representing reality, will support the new opinion and the new behavior. Otherwise, the same factors that produced the initial opinion and the behavior will continue to operate to nullify the effect of the opinion change" (Leon Festinger, "Behavioral Support for Opinion Change," *Public Opinion Quarterly*, XXVIII [Fall 1964], 416).
2. Murray G. Ross, *Community Organization* (New York: Harper and Bros., 1955), p. 40.
3. John Spencer, *Stress and Release in an Urban Estate* (London: Tavistock Publications, 1964), pp. 39–40.
4. This pressure is analyzed in a case study by Edward O. Moe, "Consulting with a Community System: A Case Study," *Journal of Social Issues*, XV, no. 2 (1959), 34.
5. Du Pont Education Committee field notes, March 13, 1963.
6. Du Pont Executive Committee field notes, May 8, 1963.
7. Ibid.
8. This statement would suggest that a tendency toward oligarchy prevails in organizations with limited resources as well as in those which have achieved a considerable measure of success. For a classical discussion of the latter condition formulated as the "iron law of oligarchy," see Robert Michels, *Political Parties* (Glencoe, Ill.: Free Press, 1949), p. 400. For a discussion of the relation of "elites" to apathy in organizations, see David Sills, *The Volunteers* (Glencoe, Ill.: Free Press, 1957), pp. 33–34.
9. Ross, *Community Organization*, p. 164.

10. One project, such as getting a new school, can contain elements of all three types of goals. The crucial factor is that a council be alert to the differences in exchanges required for the different types.
11. For a comprehensive analysis of the problems involved in project selection, see Alfred J. Kahn, *Theory and Practice of Social Planning* (New York: Russell Sage Foundation, 1969), pp. 60–129.
12. Du Pont General Meeting field notes, January 24, 1963.
13. For a discussion of the relationship between structure and the goal-attainment potentialities of organizations dedicated to bringing about social change, see Martin Rein, "Organization for Social Change," *Social Work*, IX (April 1964), 32–41.
14. For a discussion of the conflict conditions that promote the formation of interest groups like Du Pont, see Rolf Dahrendorf, *Class and Class Conflict in Industrial Society* (Stanford: Stanford University Press, 1959), pp. 180–82.
15. For a discussion of voluntary organizations and conflict situations, see Martin Rein and Robert Morris, "Goals, Structures, and Strategies of Community Change," *Social Work Practice, 1962* (New York: Columbia University Press, 1962), p. 133.
16. See note 3 of Chapter 4.
17. Hausknecht disputes this leadership-training function of voluntary organizations: "Leadership in voluntary associations may be denied to those who have not already acquired the necessary bureaucratic skills and knowledge elsewhere; instead of being the training ground for leaders, associations become the contexts for further exercise of skills learned in other spheres" (Murray Hausknecht, *The Joiners* [New York: Bedminster Press, 1962], p. 113). The Du Pont experience corroborates this idea. All but one member of the executive committee had occupations or avocations that required exercising a great deal of organizational skill.

11

Organizational Maintenance

Gordon Blackwell's observation that America is a graveyard for councils[1] dramatizes the difficulty that councils have in maintaining themselves. Stability is important not only in the obvious sense that it is necessary for carrying out long-term projects, but also because of the long-term effect a council itself can have on a neighborhood. Much of what Du Pont achieved came about because the council existed as a stable organization over a period of years, thus forcing other organizations, such as city agencies, to come to terms with it.[2]

A number of interrelated factors account for Du Pont's stability. Success in one project aided the council in others. Success ultimately led to organizational prestige, a resource that further enhanced the council's stability. The presence of the worker, who organized projects that bridged conflicts of interest, provided short-term as well as long-term rewards, and developed coalitions, was also crucial to Du Pont's stability. All these factors have already been described in detail. Other factors relating to Du Pont's stability bear further analysis.

Exchanges and Stability

Accommodations

Hill was concerned about the stability of the council, for much of his job evaluation depended on his ability to keep people involved in council activities. He assumed that the more goals the council could achieve, the more stable and powerful it would become. Although some degree of project success is obviously vital for council stability, his assumption is an oversimplification. There are many ways to achieve any one goal, and some are better suited than others for promoting the stability of the organization.

For example, at an executive committee meeting a member mentioned that some local residents had become alarmed over the reduction in the number of police in the area. All present felt that this cutback was not good, especially since the approaching summer months were usually periods of heightened tension. After gathering the consensus of the group, the chairman suggested that a letter be sent to the precinct captain, asking for a meeting. He then asked for volunteers to serve on the delegation. At this point a member raised his hand and asked, "Do you want to activate the police, or do you want to activate the council?" He wanted to secure a delegation of people from the neighborhood to be chosen at a public meeting.

There were, no doubt, several reasons why the committee did not accept his suggestion and sent its own delegation.[3] One was the false assumption that what is good for the neighborhood is good for council maintenance. This supposition is also an oversimplification. Although on countless occasions during the year the council was given a respectful hearing by city officials and surprisingly often got what it wanted, it never acquired members, commitment, or money commensurate with its efforts. What Du Pont did accomplish with the precinct captain was a stable exchange. He supplied more police, and the council gave him generalized support, or at least did not criticize him to his superiors.[4] If all a council had to do would be to achieve such limited goals, this kind of accommodation would be functional. However, a council must also recruit resources from any one project for its future projects.

The member who referred to activating the police was pointing to a conflict between rewards. On the one hand, a council must produce rewards for organizations whose cooperation it needs—and hence not unduly criticize them—and, on the other hand, it must create rewards for its potential members by making them aware of a problem and showing them what they can do about it. Therefore, a council must give careful consideration to the way in which it carries out projects. Those methods most likely to promote its ability to enter into continuing and future exchanges are best suited for maintaining council stability. Yet accommodations are not always to the good, especially when they prevent councils from entering into controversy.

Commitment and Solidarity

Hill was aware that the best hope for making the council more stable was increasing the commitment of its members.[5] He relied on project involvement as the major technique of creating binding exchanges between the council and its members. However, since this technique does not necessarily secure commitment beyond the immediate project, sole reliance on it has limitations. When such danger signs as a drop-off in attendance and apathy toward the organization begin to crop up in a council, the search for new projects to spur commitment can be self-defeating. Lack of commitment is only in part caused by a shortage of projects. It is also caused by a failure to develop other bases and processes through which binding exchanges are made.

James Coleman notes that some people form attachments on the basis of ideas and values, some on the basis of personal relationships, and others on the basis of group loyalties.[6] His statement indicates that commitment may be developed in several ways. When a council relies exclusively on appeals to norms of citizen participation and on the actual involvement of people working on problems as the only methods of developing commitment, it is being shortsighted; for those people who do not form commitments on the basis of ideas and values are in general overlooked by these methods. If, for example, working-class Puerto Ricans form commitments on the basis of their loyalty to their ethnic group, then a council seeking the commitment of Puerto Ricans might consider ways of gaining the support of the Puerto Rican group. This might involve electing a Puerto Rican officer of the council or organizing the Puerto Ricans into groups of their own.

There are other reasons why involvement at formal meetings alone is a poor mechanism for achieving commitment. One is the time interval between meetings. Du Pont's general membership meetings were held once a month, as were the health and education meetings. Often a month went by without contact among members; thus the chances of learning about the council's purposes and procedures were lessened. In contrast, the sports committee met formally almost every week during the year, as well as informally on the ballfield or the basketball court.[7] The high attendance at regular weekly meetings played a major part in the committee's development of a well-articulated set of norms, which promoted solidarity and commitment. In no other committee was there such commitment and solidarity of purpose.

One requisite for a dedicated membership is that members know what they can and cannot do in the context of the council. Unfulfilled and unrealistic expectations can be disasterous. A council must develop means of socializing members to its overall values, as well as articulate ways by which members can learn to perform organizational roles. The idea that attitudes and values can be learned simply by letting people come to committee meetings and participate in any activity they desire is refuted by the fact that people in Du Pont who randomly attended a meeting, more often than not, did not return.[8]

Goal achievement is not the sole function of meetings for organizations. The Town Hall meeting on delinquency was a significant event in the history of Du Pont. It was essentially symbolic and ceremonial, for no decisions or plans were made; yet it brought the council new members, provided it with influence over the political clubs, and gave it an image of power. Had Hill been more aware of the limitations of small committee meetings, he might have utilized mass meetings or other types of ceremonial events to develop the commitment and the solidarity that the council needed.

There was also a lack of awareness in Du Pont of the necessity to develop expressive symbols. For example, at a going-away dinner for three members of the executive committee, one of the founders of the council, in accepting his gift, praised the council for having had in eight years only three such award nights. He noted that Du Pont produced results whereas other councils merely produced awards for their members. No doubt many councils were purely expressive as he implied, but Du Pont denied its members the important social function that this type of affair can perform.

Maintaining Internal Consensus

Since Du Pont did not directly concern itself with socializing its members to norms of participation, the stability of the council is all the more surprising. Etzioni notes that organizations such as councils generally must resort to normative appeals to maintain internal harmony.[9] Although Du Pont did this, its success in preventing internal conflict was largely the result of its structural differentiation.

Discord and tension in the council was centered in the sports committee. In effect, the committee structure contained the disharmony and kept it from spreading throughout the council.[10] Instead of disrupting the council, the sports committee, as has been noted, provided the council with some of its most valuable resources for exchange. Norms of citizen participation and cooperation are not socially sanctioned to any degree in our society. So a council can seldom depend solely on appeals to these norms to maintain internal harmony and stability.

Although segregation of dissenting groups in committees does not get to the root of the discord, it can help maintain the stability of a council. Segregation is feasible to the extent that it enables dissenting groups to maximize their rewards. The sports committee remained intact because of the number of rewards its members received.

Stable Exchanges

As the sports committee attests, maintaining a certain number of stable exchanges promotes internal stability. The recurring nature of the rewards that the committee provided was important. The crucial factor lay in the continuing desire for rewards that could only be had through repeated contacts with this council committee.

There is inherent instability in a council's moving from one project to another. New exchanges have to be made as different resources are needed; rewards may not be available immediately; and costs may mount. Although a council's effectiveness is not necessarily served by establishing a stable set of exchanges, a new council, concerned about maintaining itself, would do well to consider a project that, if successful, would hold the promise of a stable set of exchanges. For example, in a case where organizational stability is the only consideration and a choice has to be made, it would be preferable for a new council to sponsor a homework-helper project rather than try to get a new school built, since there is generally only one school to be built in a neighborhood.[11]

Du Pont's stability was enhanced by its coalition, which provided many of the resources that the council needed, as well as an enduring commitment. There was a stable exchange between the council and its coalition. The experience of other HEED councils shows that it is difficult to form a coalition. Yet it seems clear that whether a council has a coalition or not, it will have an elite of some type, no matter how much it tries to broaden the involvement of participants. Whatever the form of the organization, not everyone will have both the requisites for leadership positions and a desire to hold such positions. Instead of focusing on how to maintain the total organization, a council would do better to view the problem as one of maintaining an active elite and a body of participants who are committed in varying degrees and who can be called upon when their resources are needed.

Tactics are not necessarily the same for maintaining both groups. For the elites providing opportunities for securing negotiable rewards, as Du Pont did with its opportunity ladders in education and politics, can be a stabilizing mechanism. For the general participants a council may have to provide service rewards, such as a citizen's advice bureau, or hold symbolic events, such as Town Hall meetings or parades, where rewards are available for limited participation. This concept does not mean that attempts to broaden involvement should stop or that certain participants would not be allowed to attend meetings where planning and decision-making go on. It does mean that if such efforts at broad involvement do not succeed, a council still has a way to maintain limited involvement. Since many people can be expected to want to participate only in a limited way, a council would aid its stability if it planned exchanges that are conducive to such limited participation.

The Worker and Stability

In Du Pont, Hill's job was to build a stable and effective council. A founding member of Du Pont—the one who made the distinction between activating the police and activating the council—told the researcher that building a stable council was the one job that Hill and the other Du Pont workers were not equipped to do. He contended that the Du Pont staff workers had a common failing—"They didn't know how to run an organization." In his opinion the workers did not give sufficient consideration to the organizational consequences of their actions or those of the council. He felt that the workers were more concerned with solving neighborhood problems than with building an organization capable of solving neighborhood problems. It was his contention that the organizational skills of the staff workers did not go beyond making announcements attractive, preparing precise agendas, compiling materials, thoroughly briefing chairmen, stimulating discussion, responding promptly and courteously to phone calls, making suggestions about program ideas, following through on details, etc. He felt that the council sorely needed the input of another level of organizational knowledge: how to socialize members, create symbols, develop influence, and build commitment.

Contrary to this member's opinion, Hill was extremely concerned about building a stable, effective organization capable of operating independently of him. However, he could not devise ways of countering the constraints on him to prod, backstop, stimulate programs, and maintain control. As noted, he did lack knowledge about the need to create symbols and patterns of socialization. Had he possessed such knowledge he might have had the means to counter some of the constraints on him.

Hill also lacked a means of evaluating his effect on the council, an organizational dynamic—like a concept of exchange—that would have helped him translate his actions into more effective functioning. Without ability to gauge the effects of his actions on the council, Hill had no basis upon which to develop a new role for himself. Goodenough states the case baldly when he argues the advisability of the community-development worker's assuming the role of prophet in certain situations in primitive societies. He continues, "Yet there is no reason that a secure individual who is aware of the processes at work cannot successfully utilize his clients' transference in the development situation to help them solve their dependence."[12] Essentially Goodenough is pressing for a staff worker to become a charismatic leader, to use himself as a source of reward to bring about change. He rests his case upon the principle that an organization's goals, in the reality situation in which it operates, must dictate what the worker's role should entail. In the same vein Holmberg describes a case where workers assumed an autocratic role to change an essentially dictatorial community into a democratic one.[13]

A worker will always have some kind of effect on an organization. It is his job to be able to analyze this effect and devise ways of countering it should it be detrimental to the stability and effectiveness of the organization. For example, in some organizations the worker might stay for a limited period of time. The membership would then realize some of the limits of his role; and, to an extent, his known departure date would enhance his influence as an expert on neighborhood and organizations. Knowledge of this date might also counter some of his own desires to get overly involved with particular programs, as well as minimize the constraint to prod, backstop, and assume increasing responsibility. He would have to consider ways—such as setting up opportunity ladders, developing projects with recurring rewards, and using procedures that allow limited participation—in which the organization could be stabilized after his departure, rather than simply promote goals that he considered important.

Summary

It is a moot question whether or not there should be a staff worker in neighborhood councils. Someone in a leadership role must possess the requisite knowledge about neighborhood life and about organizational functioning. Without this knowledge most councils will die; it is doubtful that many lay people will have this knowledge. More significant questions are, How long should a worker stay with a council? and How can a council's stability be ensured once a worker leaves?[14] Whether a worker remains for one year, two, or indefinitely, he must master a host of organizational skills. These include skills often depicted as necessary, for example, knowledge of group process, fund-raising, and public relations.[15] In addition, they include another level of knowledge and skill, for example, the ability to develop solidarity and commitment among members, the ability to create enduring symbols of the organization, and skill in indoctrinating members in their role and techniques of maintaining internal harmony.

Controlling one or two decisions of public institutions is not the same as exerting some type of long-term control over such institutions. In the latter case accommodations, such as occurred between Du Pont and the police, tend to take place. Since these accommodations limit the degree of control that can be imposed, staff workers should be aware of such tendencies.

NOTES

1. See note 1 of the "Introduction."
2. City agencies seem in some situations to be looking for symbols of popular support on which to base their actions.
3. It is true that such delegations create rewards, but almost all the rewards go to the delegation. The council does not automatically gain in prestige, new members, or commitment. The same people continue to get the rewards, and the chances of their tiring of such activities after a time is probable.
4. A real danger of such accommodations is that in order to maintain itself a council may lose its effectiveness as an instrument of social change. Rather than promote goals that threaten a stable set of exchanges, a council can succumb to goal displacement. See David Sills, "Voluntary Associations: In-struments and Objects of Change," *Human Organization*, XVIII (Spring 1959), 17–21.
5. For a discussion of the various types of commitment, see Helen P. Gouldner, "Dimensions of Organizational Commitment," *Administrative Science Quarterly*, IV (March 1960), 468–87.
6. Discussed by Gouldner, ibid., p. 469. Gans comments that peer groups shy away from activities that may split the group. Herbert Gans, *The Urban Villagers* (Glencoe, Ill.: Free Press, 1962), pp. 89–92.
7. There was an interesting practical reason why the sports committee met each week during the baseball season. Two new baseballs for each game during the week were distributed to the coaches. A team might not get its ball if its representative was not present.
8. Interestingly enough, early in its history through money from Jefferson House,

Du Pont sent three of its members to a course on the community and its problems given at a local university. Though, no doubt, there were other factors involved, these three members continued to be great assets to Du Pont through the years. Socialization was certainly a function of this course.

9. Amitai Etzioni, *A Comparative Analysis of Complex Organizations* (Glencoe, Ill.: Free Press, 1961), p. 44.

10. As noted earlier, there are times when structuring a committee by segregating its members becomes dysfunctional for a council.

11. The Du Pont Education Committee became unstable as soon as the replacement for PS 4 was secured.

12. Ward Hunt Goodenough, *Cooperation in Change* (New York: Russell Sage Foundation, 1963), p. 318.

13. See Allan R. Holmberg, "Participant Intervention in the Field," *Human Organization*, XIV (Spring 1955), 23–26.

14. The question of how long· a worker should remain in a neighborhood is discussed in David R. Hunter, *The Slums: Challenge and Response* (New York: Free Press, 1964), pp. 188–89.

15. See, for example, Violet M. Sieder, "What Is Community Organization Practice?" *The Social Welfare Forum, 1956*, Proceedings of the National Conference on Social Welfare (New York: Columbia University Press, 1956), pp. 167–74.

12

Neighborhoods, Politics, and Councils

THERE WERE periods in the early 1920s and shortly after the Second World War when many people felt that councils were the instrument through which the ordinary citizen could gain control over his social and physical environment. They believed that through a council grass-roots democracy could become a reality.[1] Yet neighborhood councils did not spread around the country to any great extent, and an indigenous social movement did not develop around them.

Perhaps the most basic reason for this failure lies in the nature and the scope of a neighborhood council. First the depression and then World War II emphasized the limitations of a neighborhood approach to problem-solving, for these events clearly illustrated that the locus of modern man's difficulties is not primarily centered in the neighborhood. A neighborhood council by itself could not create more jobs or stop wars, raise wages or build new housing.[2] As national and federal arrangements were increasingly made to cope with the complexity and interdependence of American life, neighborhood councils were still essentially a local approach to solving problems. However, the causes of these problems were for the most part located in systems external to and not amenable to control by local areas. As Form notes in his study of Greenbelt, Maryland, any small part of a social system, which a neighborhood is, will inevitably reflect the relationships and the problems inherent in the larger social system.[3] The implication is that solutions to most social problems do not lie in local areas.

Neighborhood Functions of Councils

Even though essential validity is granted to Form's statement, Du Pont's experience indicates that people do encounter serious problems in neighborhoods and that some actions can be taken to solve these problems at the local level. Often as is the case with race riots, problems must be handled locally, even though the long-range solution lies in the larger social order. There are potential functions that a council-like organization can perform in a neighborhood to help improve the existing social and physical conditions. Du Pont was able to perform the following functions:

1. The council assumed a watchdog function over local governmental agencies. A former youth patrolman in the area told the researcher that it was good for the local precinct to know that the council was concerned with its activities, for this knowledge kept it on its toes. The same could be said about the local parks department and the public-school officials.
2. The council was able to influence public opinion in the neighborhood concerning certain proposed solutions to neighborhood problems. It achieved this end by stating its solution and by providing people with a means of working on the solution. The prime example was the shift from the vigilante approach to delinquency to one of providing services and promoting intergroup relations.
3. The council was able to act as a neighborhood interest group and effectively claim the area's share of services from city government. It secured the renovation of Johnson Oval, a replacement for PS 4, an area services project for Harold Street, a reading-improvement clinic, additional streetlights, acceptance of its urban renewal plan, and more police protection.
4. To an extent the council increased neighborhood-mindedness among both professionals and citizens. Du Pont was the only available organization where Roman Catholics and Protestants could sit and discuss together. Staff turnover was high at many of the local agencies and organizations, and the rumbles committee provided new staff with a neighborhood orientation. The *Du Pont News* supplied general information about what was going on in the neighborhood.

5. The council provided services for the neighborhood. In the late 1950s it operated a housing clinic and provided relocation services. Hill started a homework-helper program. In addition, the newspaper was a good source of advertisement for local businessmen. The council also coordinated the efforts of local agencies to provide services that none could have offered alone, for example, the Little League and the summer program.

The Council's Relationship to the Neighborhood

Critics of neighborhood councils advance the argument that neighborhoods in an organic and integrated sense no longer have any real significance for city residents.[4] Coleman has speculated that a society may be emerging that will have social organization without local organization. For him the ecology of the city no longer conforms to neighborhood lines. He sees the power to make decisions about those things which affect neighborhoods often residing in places other than the neighborhoods and, as a result, local residents seldom developing sentiments or mutual expectations about how problems should be solved.[5]

The argument over the proper emphasis on neighborhood work in social work has had a long history. On the one hand, Robert Woods, in his influential work *Neighborhood in Nation-Building*, was a staunch advocate of promoting citizen interest in preserving socially decent neighborhoods. He coined the phrase "a strong neighborhood, a strong city, a strong country."[6] On the other hand, Jane Addams is reported to have said to a student, "Young man, I do not believe in geographical salvation."[7]

The Du Pont area in the early 1930s was an organic Italian neighborhood, integrated within itself and tied in through various links with the larger social order. In the late 1950s, it had become an area made up of diverse ethnic groups, with few internal connections and no external voice. Besides the changes in ethnic composition, another factor that further tended to break down the neighborhood was a change in the political structure. In the early 1900s each alderman (councilman) represented 47,000 people. By 1950 each councilman represented approximately 315,000 people. As a councilman's district grew in size, he became less accessible to his constituents, and they in turn became more heterogeneous. Few districts of 315,000 persons can comprise a natural neighborhood or be composed of a single ethnic group.

What occurred in the Du Pont area in the late 1950s was a convergence of interests among various groups. The ministers, social workers,

Negroes, Jews, and Puerto Ricans found that they had common concerns in the schools, public safety, and recreation. Out of these common concerns the Du Pont Council developed. To an extent the desire to control local conditions created the new neighborhood's identity. Control of the old neighborhood had been founded on different bases.

Contrary to Louis Wirth's classic "Urbanism as a Way of Life,"[8] urbanism in the middle 1960s was many ways of life. The Du Pont experience indicates that although the organic neighborhoods seemed to be breaking down in our cities, locality factors in such traditional neighborhoods were still affecting people's lives in significant ways. Although previous arguments over the place of social work or community organization in neighborhoods have revolved around the creation of organic neighborhoods modeled after small towns, Du Pont was pointing to a new direction. Rather than to attempt to recreate such neighborhoods, which were created by factors that in the main no longer exist, the function of community organization is to develop new forms of internal and external integration relative to the conditions that exist. Du Pont did this task through such tactics as creating the Little League, ensuring that the neighborhood had representation on the local school board, opening the political clubhouse to Negroes and Puerto Ricans, and decreasing racial conflict.

Functions Not Performed by the Council

There are functions often claimed for neighborhood councils that Du Pont did not perform. It did not attempt to integrate the neighborhood around itself (as the town meeting tended to do in colonial New England) by setting itself up as a quasi-neighborhood legislature. It took into account already existing organizational patterns of local decision-making and attempted to bring about changes in these patterns. Much of Du Pont's success was due to the fact that many vital functions were not being performed for the neighborhood by existing organizations. The council, for example, made the local political clubs start to function as an interest group for the neighborhood. Presumably, if the clubs had already been performing this function, Du Pont would have been less successful in this area. By gearing itself to activate dormant functions of existing structures, Du Pont met less resistance from these structures than it would have had if it had attempted to usurp the functions. This strategy enabled the council to promote citizen participation outside the confines of the council in such places as the political clubs and the parents' associations.

The council operated on the principle that in order to promote the democratization of other structures, it was not necessary that all organizations, including itself, rigidly adhere to democratic procedures.[9] The council recognized that its own leadership had to do more than clearly present the council's point of view. The council had to have a way of gaining compliance other than by simply making appeals on the basis of the common good. Thus Du Pont did not elect, but selected its chairman. Elections were pro forma. It purported to speak for the neighborhood when it really represented a coalition that was more interested in getting its point of view across than carrying out its internal activities in a democratic fashion. In this sense of representing a coalition's point of view, Du Pont was an effective political tool.

Councils as Political Tools

The fact that Du Pont was founded and nourished mainly by Protestant ministers is important not only for understanding the council but also for understanding its relationship to politics. It was in the middle 1950s, concurrent with the founding of Du Pont, that the Protestant clergy, under the threat of empty churches, rediscovered the inner-city parish and began redefining its relationship to the political powers. Harvey Cox illustrates this redefinition when he states, "In a city, the way a neighborhood is best maintained, especially where the vast majority of people do not own their own homes, has more to do with learning how to apply political pressure on landlords than with learning how to apply putty with a knife."[10] The creating of neighborhood-based organizations of citizens, politically nonpartisan, was the tactic the clergy chose to implement their new point of view.

The lack of support for Du Pont among the Italians, as well as among the working-class residents in general, is understandable. Du Pont was derived from the middle-class ethos and favored what the classical municipal reform movement defined as "good government"—efficiency, impartiality, planning, strict enforcement of laws, etc.[11] The Italian and working-class political style was close to "the other conception of the public interest (one never explicitly formulated as such but one all the same). . . . This is the conception of those people who . . . look to politician for help and favors, regard gambling and vice as, at worst, necessary evils and who are far less interested in the efficiency and impartiality of local government than in its readiness to confer material benefits of one sort or another on them."[12]

Although OPUS was correct in its disagreement with HEED in predicting that a council like Du Pont would not attract large numbers of working-class people, it underestimated the political utility of councils. OPUS assumed, first, that a council must operate according to the classical form of democratic procedure rather than be controlled by a powerful coalition. Secondly, it overlooked the fact that when there are no organizations concerned with particular spheres of public interest, almost any organization who cares to can garner considerable influence in that sphere. Thirdly, it underestimated the ability of a council to develop tactics for engaging in conflict, that is, neutralizing the opposition or keeping it disorganized. Fourthly, it assumed that political power is solely rooted in the actuality of large numbers of people or large amounts of money. It overlooked the importance of the perceptions or image of an organization in relation to its power. Banfield and Wilson note that the process of political learning consists, in great part, of imputing to certain people, organizations, ideas, or strategies those qualities which make them important to everyone involved in politics. This concept does not imply that the important things about city politics are figments of the imagination of the people concerned. It only argues that politics takes place in a world compounded not only of hard facts (material stakes in certain issues, unmistakable legal or economic powers and sanctions, clear instances of influence being wielded) but also of cultural artifacts (learned responses, shared vocabulary, general expectations, and imputed reputations).[13]

Many city departments perceived HEED as a powerful organization. Du Pont skillfully utilized its connection with HEED to enhance its own ends and ultimately was itself perceived as a powerful organization. OPUS overlooked a change in the style and requisites of city politics. City departments staffed by professionals often need access to community groups outside of the usual party lines. The planning professionals in the city planning department were glad to have the support of Du Pont in developing an urban renewal plan for the area. By setting itself up as the voice of the people, Du Pont helped the city planners legitimize their plans and counter proposals from other sources.

Du Pont was deeply enmeshed in the political life of the neighborhood. If Banfield and Wilson are correct in asserting that a shift is occurring from a predominantly lower-class to a predominantly middle-class political style, then nonparty lines of access to city administration may become increasingly important, that is, newspapers, business groups, churches, and neighborhood councils.[14]

Neighborhood councils are very much in the middle-class, Protestant style of politics. The Du Pont experience shows that in a neighborhood where a coalition of interests can be developed, councils can be effective political tools. Yet councils are not an alternative to politics, for they cannot resolve disagreement and conflict and institute rationalism and efficiency. Instead, they can be considered as a middle-class tool that can be useful in gaining local consensus about political issues and can, with sophisticated leadership, possess considerably more potential for engaging in controversial issues than was thought possible prior to this study.

Summary

In creating new forms of neighborhood integration, Du Pont did not attempt to integrate the neighborhood around itself. Instead, the council used itself to foster the integration into the neighborhood of other systems, such as the schools, politics, and housing. Much of the traditional thinking about councils has implied that a council should become the focal point of neighborhood life, as was the town meeting in the small town. The Du Pont experience contradicts this emphasis and points the way toward a more delimited use of councils as organizational tools for affecting various neighborhood social systems.

Recently advocates of community control have added a new dimension to the discussion of the quality of life in urban slum neighborhoods and communities. Plans for localized economic development and taxing schemes have been formulated. Demands for local control of all public institutions have been articulated. In the epilogue the utility of these ideas will be discussed in the light of Du Pont's experience.

NOTES

1. See, for example, Violet M. Sieder, "Solving Health and Welfare Problems Through Neighborhood Participation," *The Social Welfare Forum, 1951*, Proceedings of the National Conference on Social Welfare (New York: Columbia University Press, 1951), pp. 311–22.
2. Dennis claims that the emphasis on that part which locality factors play in the etiology of social and personal problems is politically conservative and serves to inhibit questions about the larger social arrangements. N. Dennis, "Popularity of the Neighborhood Community Idea," *Sociological Review, VI* (December 1958), 202.
3. William H. Form, "Status Stratification in a Planned Community," *American Sociological Review, X* (October 1945), 612.
4. For the classic statement of the neighborhood concept in city planning and

social work, see Ernest W. Burgess, "The Natural Area as the Unit for Social Work in the Large City," *Proceedings of the National Conference of Social Work* (Chicago: University of Chicago Press, 1926), and Clarence A. Perry, "Neighborhood Planning from the Social Viewpoint," *Proceedings of the National Conference of Social Work* (Chicago: University of Chicago Press, 1924). For a critical analysis of this concept, see Reginald Isaacs, "The Neighborhood Concept in Theory and Application," *Land Economics*, XXV (February 1949), 73–78, and Leo Kuper, "Social Science Research and the Planning of Urban Neighborhoods," *Social Forces*, XXXIX (March 1951), 237–43.

5. James S. Coleman, "Community Disorganization," *Contemporary Social Problems*, ed. Robert K. Merton and Robert Nisbet (New York: Harcourt, Brace & World, 1961), p. 576.

6. Robert A. Woods, *Neighborhood in Nation-Building* (Cambridge, Mass.: Houghton Mifflin Co., 1923), p. 9.

7. Jane Addams, as quoted by Margaret Berry in "The Contributions of the Neighborhood Approach in Solving Today's Problems," *Social Service Review*, XXXVI (June 1962), 190.

8. In *American Journal of Sociology*, 44 (July 1938).

9. Conservative politicians have long argued for the abolition of unions on the basis that they were not democratic, did not have real elections with opposition parties and candidates, and tended to autocratic leadership. Although at this point it is debatable how much internal conflict and disagreement a union can tolerate, clearly the union movement could never have been organized without a great deal of internal control and discipline among the members. Rigid adherence to democratic procedure would have weakened the unions to such a point that they could not have supported the interests of their members. The stability of our democracy and the allegiance of the working class might well have been weakened. For a general discussion of procedures in voluntary organizations, as well as a specific statement about the above point, see Avery Leiserson, "Problems of Representation in the Government of Private Groups," *Journal of Politics*, XI (August 1949), 66–77, and Zecharia Chafee, "The Internal Affairs of Associations Not for Profit," *Harvard Law Review*, XLIII (May 1930), 993–1029.

10. Harvey Cox, *The Secular City* (New York: Macmillan, 1965), p. 140.

11. Richard Hofstadter, *The Age of Reform* (New York: Alfred Knopf, 1955), p. 9. It should be noted that although the Protestant political ethic is moralistic and individualistic, Protestants also tend to act as other ethnic groups do in seeking and maintaining political power.

12. Edward C. Banfield and James Q. Wilson, *City Politics* (Cambridge: Harvard University Press and M.I.T. Press, 1963), p. 46.

13. Ibid., pp. 58–59.

14. Ibid., p. 333.

Part IV

Epilogue

13

Du Pont:
Five Years After

As I walked down Great Street one day in the spring of 1969, looking up I suddenly realized that staring across at each other were the twentieth story of Brown Houses, a public housing project, and the cross on top of St. Catherine's Catholic Church. Somehow I had never noticed them. Outwardly the neighborhood had changed little since the summer of 1964 when I had left it. There was the new school for which the council had successfully agitated. And just to the north of Du Pont the replacement for the old Dutch Hospital was in construction. My favorite coffee shop was gone, replaced by a pizzeria.

Inside, the council office seemed more cluttered than usual with maps and letters and pictures of former events. A noticeable change was the masthead of the most recent issue of the *Du Pont News*, as well as the format of its pages. One of the oldest members of the council told me a few days later that the *News* had a "hippie format" and was not well received in the community. Another old member told me that Du Pont was no longer a neighborhood council, that it did not represent the neighborhood but was now merely an adjunct of the Poverty Program.

Du Pont from 1964 to 1969

A brief history of the council's activities during the five years after the study will provide a basis for judging the accuracy of their comments.[1]

1964–1965

In the fall of 1964 Martin Hill resigned as worker at Du Pont to become director of HEED and was succeeded by a recent social work graduate, Nassau Paulman. As Hill was extremely well liked in the council, especially by its chairman, Paulman had a difficult time gaining acceptance. The chairman, active in the council since its inception in 1955, had a long history of berating professionals even before this practice became popular in the Poverty Program. In 1963, before he was elected chairman, he had publicly berated Hill for his inefficiency and incompetence.

Paulman, in turn, pursued much the same policy as did Hill. He went to all the sports committee meetings and took minutes. He realized that if he was to maintain his position in the council, he would have to gain the acceptance of the sports committee members, as well as of the council chairman, who had been instrumental in founding the committee.

Paulman quickly went to work on the *Du Pont News*. Through his efforts in gaining ads from large department stores, the *News* was expanded to eight pages. He tried to work in the area of urban renewal, but there seemed little that he could do to speed the slow-moving urban renewal plan through the government bureaucracy. Paulman needed to achieve something quite substantial in the council to solidify his own position. Each of the preceding staff workers had brought to the council a particular area of expertise and interest; Paulman needed to do the same. The state of education in the local schools provided him with such an opportunity.

Through money provided in 1964 by OPUS, Du Pont had administered a summer reading program for elementary school children. However, as fall approached, the education committee had no really significant program objectives. In addition, as the months passed, Paulman became increasingly disappointed with the level of its discussions, which he characterized as "lace tea doilies at parent-teacher teas." Therefore, in late winter he set about organizing an educational task force composed of paid agency personnel from the churches and Jefferson House and of community people, most of whom were not members of the education committee.

This group drew up a proposal for an expanded summer reading program. It was to be funded through the Poverty Program, which in early 1965 was in a state of administrative chaos. Lines of authority and responsibility were unclear, and program priorities were unavailable. This situation proved to be beneficial for the council and for Paulman. Since local agencies made up the task force that was working on the proposal, these organizations were deeply invested in the reading program. With the school year coming to a conclusion and the bureaucracy unable to move on the program, Paulman was able to mount a quickly organized march on City Hall of well over 200 people. This demonstration, plus other pressure tactics, ultimately brought success and at the same time stirred up a great deal of enthusiasm for the reading program in the neighborhood. The council received a grant of $109,000 to provide reading assistance to 300 children during the summer. Paulman was clearly the architect of this victory and threw a party in his apartment to celebrate the event. After this achievement his position in the council was secure.

1965–1966

The major innovation in the expanded reading program lay in the hiring of mothers to help the teachers with the summer reading classes. Paulman believed that these women could be of use during the school year also, and he did not want to lose contact with them. However, he felt that the education committee did not provide the type of opportunities for participation that would maintain their commitment: the committee had a well-ordered routine that did not require large numbers of members to participate actively. It met monthly with the local superintendent, held periodic workshops about school affairs, etc.

He, therefore, reconvened his task force and through it developed a proposal for a parent-development program. This program was geared to such areas as acquainting parents with the workings of the school, apprising them of their children's rights in relation to school, and assisting them in helping with homework. A grant of $60,000 from the Office of Economic Opportunity was received in January of 1966 for the program. Three coordinators were hired—one Chinese, one Puerto Rican, and one Negro.

Relations between the council and the schools were still excellent as witnessed by this letter in the October, 1965, issue of the *Du Pont News:*

It is with great anticipation that we at Charles Sumner Junior High School look forward to the year's first issue of the *Du Pont News*. . . . The excellent handling of noteworthy community news by your organization is well recognized by all. I speak not only of the coverage afforded the summer activities, but also to the coverage given to all of our other community agencies. . . . Again, best wishes for a successful year.

John H. Gold, Principal,
Charles Sumner Junior High School.

This was to be the last year of cordial relationships between the council and the local schools.

The sports committee, which had carried out a successful program in 1965, repeated the performance in 1966. Parades grew larger each year, as did the number of boys enrolled on the teams. Yet by 1966 the seeds of decline were apparent. The Poverty Program was operating at full force. More and more stridently, the coaches—especially from the Roman Catholic organizations—verbalized their complaint, "Why coach for nothing?"

By 1966 Paulman attended sports committee meetings only sporadically. When he did, he was met repeatedly with the accusation, "You spend all your time doing other things." The visibility of blacks and Puerto Ricans in the neighborhood was becoming more apparent. Some 400 parents, mostly black and Puerto Rican, attended a graduation ceremony for the 1966 summer reading program. No longer could the sports committee parade claim to be the only major public event in the neighborhood.

1966–1967

No one in the council expected that the sports committee would disintegrate as quickly as it did. There had always been strain, but the situation looked promising in 1967. The new chairman of the council was an Italian who had been one of the founding members of the sports committee. Over the years he had gradually broadened his activities in the council so he seemed the perfect person to maintain integration with the sports committee. In addition, not only had the baseball league been expanded, but an extremely large and successful basketball league had been conducted during the fall and winter months.

Nevertheless, a number of factors combined to weaken the committee: a change of priests at the major Catholic church and internal feuding among members of its men's club that sponsored the ball teams intensified the conflict over free coaching. The father put certain restrictions on the use of funds by the men's club. In addition, council activities in education gave rise to the charge that Du Pont was "too far left." Also, with the presence of Vista volunteers on the staff of the local settlement house and other college volunteers in the Protestant churches, the composition of the sports committee changed dramatically. Most coaches were no longer residents of the neighborhood. Some of the coaches from the Catholic institutions seemed to view the Vistas as paid personnel, and the idea that people were getting paid to coach the teams infuriated them.

Finally, after much haranguing during the early months of 1967, it was agreed that, rather than hiring umpires from outside the neighborhood, local people would be hired and paid to umpire the games. This compromise seemed to work, but there was a drop-off in the number of teams entered in the leagues. In addition, a key member of the committee, one of the Count's lieutenants, dropped out of the committee. One factor, according to Paulman, was that a close friend of his did not receive a job in the summer reading program.

The activities of the council in relation to education during 1966 and 1967 had profound effects on the structure and composition of Du Pont. Parents once again had assisted in the summer reading program. Paulman continued to feel that these same parents could be valuable in the school during the year. His task force developed a proposal for teacher-assistants to work as remedial-reading teachers to help classroom teachers. The proposal was sent to the board of education, and ultimately after a series of sit-ins and demonstrations it was funded. Twenty local women were hired by the board of education to serve as teacher-assistants. Once again this achievement was heralded as a great triumph for the council. Indeed, this teacher-assistant program was the first in the city and was destined to be copied throughout the educational system.

The parent development program continued during 1966 and 1967, although it had begun to develop something of a controversial reputation. When it had forms printed and distributed to parents to be filled out in case their children were subjected to physical abuse in the schools, the school personnel complained bitterly through the parents' associations.

The parent development program (PDP) was governed by a board made up of local citizens of all ethnic persuasions. A crisis in the program occurred in January 1967 when one of the three coordinators, a Negro, was fired for incompetence. Most of the Negro members of the board had backed the program director in firing this particular coordinator. Unfortunately, Rev. Mr. Older's replacement, a Negro, was the only board member who did not back the dismissal. He charged racial discrimination. A public meeting was held in which various accusations were hurled. Haplessly, the program director of PDP came to the meeting two hours late. Although his late arrival was inadvertent, it tended to give credence to the charges.

The board held firm to its decision. A few months later, when a training session on "what it feels like to be black in the public school system" was held, a loud and angry picket line composed of blacks and whites marched around the training site, carrying signs "Prevent Racist Workshops." During the next week rumors of violence flooded the neighborhood. Significantly, Rev. Mr. Older, who was no longer directing his church but lived in the neighborhood, was on the picket line. (The discharged coordinator had been a secretary in his church.) Local schoolteachers were also on the line. The community was split.

Although the council served merely as a conduit for funds for PDP, it was, nevertheless, associated in the minds of most people as synonymous with it. Paulman had attempted to make a separation between PDP and the education committee, feeling that the militancy of PDP would ultimately redound to the detriment of Du Pont. The distinction he attempted to make did not hold, and his fears proved correct.

Partly in response to this situation and in order to get funds to develop other areas of the council's program, Paulman and several key members of the executive committee who felt similarly threatened by the situation decided to approach a private funding source, the Cord Foundation, for a grant. They were given a respectful hearing but were told that the foundation was interested only in funding projects related to education. The foundation was, however, impressed by Du Pont's activities in education and, in fact, was looking for a community in which to fund an experimental school decentralization project. In the spring of 1967 Du Pont received a planning grant to develop a proposal for a model school decentralized district. The educational task force was expanded to include teachers and principals to draw up the plan. Paulman felt that the planning grant could be used as an integrating device. The results turned out differently.

1967–1968

In the fall of 1967 Paulman left Du Pont to return to school. The council was unable to secure a worker for almost six months, and during this period activities were sharply curtailed. The chairman and a few loyal workers attempted to hold committee meetings and to put out the newspaper. There were several executive committee meetings, and two issues of the newspaper were published.

Strains with PDP became greater. The council chairman was anxious that the council remain a device for bringing all members of the community together. However, the parent development program, operated by its own governing board, was not concerned about the ramifications of its actions on the council. In addition, the focus of concern in the neighborhood shifted to the election of the board of the model school district. The ten members who were elected to the board consisted of a parent from each of the participating schools, a community representative, and four teachers. The election caused further strain, for the conflict over the firing of the PDP board coordinator was carried over to this election. A district director was hired, as well as a staff of curriculum and program advisers. At this point the model school district became a legal entity on its own apart from Du Pont.

When Unhan, the new worker, came in February of 1968 he found a considerably weakened council. Before he could make an appraisal of the situation, events ran away from him. The old leadership—in one final attempt to maintain the council as the site for all ethnic groups to work together on community problems—using the rhetoric of the Poverty Program, suggested that PDP become independent. This separation took place but did not have the hoped-for result: that the council would be seen as a neutral ground for all groups. Instead, the council came to be viewed by PDP adherents as a do-nothing organization, but by PDP opponents as closely allied to PDP.

The old leadership also hoped to reactivate the sports committee, but they were unable to achieve this. The composition of the committee had significantly changed; few of the older members remained. In addition, two incidents occurred which made the 1968 season the last in which the sports committee functioned as a league of local institutions. During the parade members of one of the Catholic churches moved to the front of the line of march as the parade turned into an almost all Italian street. This action was interpreted by members of the Protestant, predominantly Negro, teams as an attempt to "put them down." After the parade the white coach explained that his boys could get more money if they were at the head of the parade. In years gone by, to avoid such problems, numbers had been drawn from a hat to determine the lead group in the parade. With the change in composition of the membership, this procedure had been overlooked.

The bitterness over the parade did not subside. A few weeks later one of the Catholic teams charged that a Negro player on another team was over age. The boy was disqualified from playing. At the next meeting of the sports committee the coaches got into a heated argument. Once again the norms about following rules and the procedures for adjudicating disputes had been forgotten. The new coaches were young and had no remembrance of prior sports committees. They were not willing to accept the vote of the majority. Finally, one of the Negro coaches stood up and said, "Du Pont is a racist organization."

The league finished out the season with a small number of teams. Some of the organizations had to combine their teams in order to continue. The sports committee was no longer able to serve a function as a meeting ground between working-class, adult men, black and white; was no longer able to unite the community; and was no longer able to serve as a resource to Du Pont on which it could borrow and pyramid additional resources.

1968–1969

The controversy over PDP had one final crucial effect on Du Pont. For the first time, in June of 1968 an election to the council chairmanship was hotly contested. The factions in the neighborhood poured into the meeting. Ultimately, a Negro woman was elected chairman. This was the first time that a chairman's election actually had been contested. The year before the Italian chairman had been induced to stay on for a third year in order to forestall such a controversial election. A Negro woman relatively unknown to the white groups could not unite the community. The only Negro whom the old leadership would have considered for chairman was one known and respected in the Italian community.

Another event that occurred in 1968 further gave the council an image of a black-dominated organization. The board of the model school district fired a Jewish principal and replaced him with a black woman. The PTA of that school, composed primarily of black, Chinese, and Puerto Rican women, was angered by this dismissal and supported the Jewish principal. Although the council and the model school district were no longer directly related, they appeared in the eyes of many as one and the same.

In addition, a satellite organization of the Cord Foundation gave a grant to the council for a program called Operation Outreach. In this program parents were paid a stipend to attend training sessions related to issues of decentralization in community-controlled schools. Sixty people were paid a stipend of $20 a week each to attend these sessions. This program gained a reputation in the neighborhood of being predominantly black oriented, and yet in the Du Pont neighborhood Negroes represented at most one-tenth of the population.[2]

In the spring of 1969 the activities of the sports committee were taken over by the area youth team, a group made up of paid staff and Vista volunteers of the local Protestant churches and Jefferson House, plus representatives from the Irish-dominated Catholic church. A baseball league was organized on a completely different basis than in the past. Teams were made up from a list of boys who signed up; age and ability were the criteria. There were no institutional teams, and the number of whites was miniscule compared with previous years—less than 10 percent. The sports parade had to be called off due to lack of interest.

As noted, the masthead for the *Du Pont News* was changed. Unhan, the new worker, had not considered the ramifications of selecting an editor, and at his urging a Negro minister was selected. Only the housing committee had any resemblance to the past functioning of the council. Over the years the housing committee had met regularly to press the city on the urban renewal plan and to deal with various other matters related to housing. As were all prior workers, Unhan was anxious to establish an area of expertise and achievement for himself. Housing appeared to be a promising area.

In 1968 funds had been granted by the federal government for a final rendering of the plans for the urban renewal site. This event considerably activated the housing committee, which acted as a watchdog on the firm doing the planning. In addition, new federal funds were available for the development of scatter-site housing by local nonprofit housing corporations. Unhan secured the cooperation of the planning department of a local university, which supplied students to develop scatter-site plans. At the time of this writing the housing committee remains the only committee dominated by the old leadership, primarily Jewish and Italian.

The other new activity developed by Unhan was a manpower program. Recruitment for training programs in clerical and office machine work was carried out in the neighborhood. Approximately one hundred people were placed in these programs. Of these the vast majority were blacks and Puerto Ricans.

At this writing Unhan views the council as an instrument for transferring power over community institutions and services from those who have it to those who do not. He feels that, because of the conflicts in the community, it is impossible for an organization to get people to come together and plan together. Although Du Pont had always had the goal of transferring power and control, there was a striking difference between 1964 and 1969. An analysis of the new exchanges made between individuals and organizations in Du Pont during these years illuminates this difference.

The New Exchanges

The major organizational problem described in prior chapters was the necessity for Du Pont to develop the rewards it needed to exchange for the resources it needed to achieve organizational ends. The first ten years of Du Pont's existence were characterized by a variety of innovative exchanges. Rewards were offered through the newspaper for resources useful in achieving educational and political ends. Similarly, the sports committee offered a range of emotional, negotiable, and ideological rewards that were used to recruit resources, some of which were used to promote ends other than sports. To a great extent Du Pont's survival and success can be directly related to exchanges developed by creating opportunity ladders, imposing costs for nonparticipation, pyramiding resources, and the like.

Du Pont never had a large membership. One reason why it did not seriously have to attempt to organize numbers of people in the community was the fact that it had a paid staff worker. This worker represented a tremendous input of resources—resources that were paid for by monetary rewards that the council did not have to create. HEED paid the worker's salary.

The major change in Du Pont between 1965 and 1969 was the multiplication of other resources for which the council did not have to provide rewards. Not only was HEED paying for one staff worker but by 1969 was paying for two, as well as for the rent of the council office and for various program expenses. Moreover, the agencies in the neighborhood had an increased number of staff people, mainly Vista volunteers, to be assigned to the work of the council. In addition to all this came the Poverty Program, offering many resources that a sophisticated worker such as Paulman could easily recruit. In 1964 Du Pont was operating on a budget of less than $10,000. By 1968 it was operating programs in excess of $200,000.

Given this surplus of resources, the necessity for maintaining the sports committee in its old structure was no longer so vital, the UNICEF carnival and Brotherhood Week seemed like trivial programs, and the significance of a relatively unknown black woman, no matter how talented, as chairman of the council was hardly noticed. The introduction of monetary rewards into the sports committee quickly corroded the ideological, emotional, and service rewards that had been intricately built up over the years. The truth that "volunteers and paid staff doing the same thing cannot operate on the same committee"—a coach's statement made in 1963—became apparent.

There were three major factors that account for the dramatic changes in Du Pont. First, the coalition organizations that maintained control over Du Pont served primarily blacks, Puerto Ricans, and Chinese. Secondly, the staff workers, Hill and Paulman, saw themselves as the spokesmen for these groups. And thirdly, large sums of money could be secured without involving white ethnic groups in the neighborhood.[3] By 1969 Unhan said that he "no longer saw any need to foster commitment in the council." He viewed the council as an organization that would start activities and then spin them off under the auspices of citizens' groups outside of the council where they, in his words, "would really be under community control." Thus, the Italians and Jews were no longer needed.

Although some of the old leadership, such as Rev. Mr. Older and Mr. Smitz, had left the neighborhood, those who remained were generally angry, confused, and nostalgic. Perhaps the most perceptive of these old-timers remarked that the council had always been an elitist organization, and, therefore, had never developed the support and following of large numbers of people in the white community, who might have had a stake in the council. Had their support been gained, they might have made an effort to maintain some control over it. He would not venture his opinion as to whether the council's change would be beneficial to the neighborhood.

Summary

By mid-1969 Du Pont was in fact an adjunct of the Poverty Program, operating in its style and rhetoric. The old council had tried to make local institutions and services responsive to the needs of all groups. It had sought to achieve this by creating subtle exchanges that it manipulated to its advantage. By community control the new council meant administrative control of local institutions primarily by black, Puerto Rican, and Chinese groups. In addition, it was able to recruit valuable resources for the furtherance of such ends without entering into exchanges for them with other groups.

Preceding chapters have utilized the exchange model to analyze various aspects of Du Pont's functioning. In conclusion, the next and last chapter will suggest, on the basis of the model, what the problems and potentialities of the council's latest espousal of community control are.

NOTES

1. Data for this and the concluding chapter were gathered from interviews with key members of the council.
2. Attendance at council committee meetings tended to reflect this new program, as well as the new composition of the sports committee. Vista volunteers and paid trainees and staff were much in evidence.
3. Most striking is the fact that the Count could not affect the distribution of poverty funds in the Du Pont neighborhood.

14

Community Control:
Rhetoric and Reality

THE OLD Du Pont Council had represented an attempt to control community services and activities by a coalition of white-dominated institutions that sought to serve the interests of black and Puerto Rican people. Its aim was to give the blacks and Puerto Ricans a share in services that were available, as well as a share in shaping policies governing these services. Its role was really that of the liberal integrationist. Brotherhood Week was its true symbol.

The new Du Pont Council remained a coalition of these selfsame organizations, concerned not so much with integration as with vigorous promotion of the rights and needs of nonwhite populations, including their right to administrative control of the services that they utilized in the neighborhood. Advising, cajoling, and threatening the bureaucracy were discarded as tactics in favor of an all-inclusive administrative control.

Both councils have used the rhetoric of community control and democratic participation as justification for their programs. The old council had used it as a tactic; the new council has taken it as a tenet and a matter of belief. This blind adherence has already created problems for the new Du Pont Council and can be expected to hamper its work further in the future.

The Rhetoric of Community Control

Much of the rhetoric of those who advocate community control is strikingly similar to the rhetoric of what has been described earlier as the ideal "community organization process." This process is essentially a rational problem-solving process in which there is complete and open sharing of all information and facts, full discussion, and ultimate decision-making on the part of everyone in the community, in terms of the best interests of the community. Indeed, this process is the ideal democratic procedure taught in any high school civics course.

A great deal of the criticism of existing community corporations and community-action organizations in the Poverty Program has been centered on the fact that "the people" have not really been involved in organizing the programs, that the downtown staff "forces programs down the throats of local communities," and that sufficient time is not allowed for the community to evolve adequate plans and procedures.[1] Advocates of community control imply that if only the people were adequately involved, there would be effective local institutions and effective community problem-solving. These advocates have returned to the old shibboleth "if goals are not achieved it is because the process was not followed." The major argument of this study is that the exchanges that occur during community problem-solving and community action have a significant effect on the outcome of such activities. The events surrounding the development of the Du Pont Model School District clearly illustrate this point.

Exchanges in the Model School District

During the spring of 1967 Paulman held a number of meetings with the staff of the Cord Foundation. By late spring an agreement was reached that Du Pont would receive a planning grant from Cord to develop a comprehensive plan for a model school district. Paulman quickly moved to set up a planning committee that would be representative of all elements in the community, as well as the teachers and the principals. Its composition included representatives from the parents' associations, teachers in the local schools, a representative of the community at large, and one of the local school principals. A more representative group could not have been developed. In addition, members of the community were kept aware of what the planning group was considering and were asked for their suggestions through innumerable community meetings.

The committee was chaired by a local Presbyterian minister. It took all of his sophistication to overcome dissension and gain consensus among the varying interests that soon emerged in the planning committee. The teachers tended to define most issues as being within their own area of competence and outside that of community people. Hostilities emerged between those who had sided with PDP in the firing of the Negro coordinator and those who had opposed it. Other conflicts arose between those who had long experience serving on the boards of the parents' associations and those who did not.

In the fall of 1967 an election was held for the governing board of the model school district. Parents were to be elected from each school, plus four teachers and one representative of the community. Only parents who had children in a particular school could vote for the representative from that school. Following the election a district administrator and a small staff of curriculum, personnel, and pupil-service technicians were hired. Unfortunately, the first district administrator proved unequal to the task of working with the board. He conveyed the idea that the board was to act as a rubber stamp for his activities. In a few months he was discharged without much fanfare in the community.

A new administrator was hired during the summer of 1968. However, he inherited a difficult situation. A total citywide school strike had been brewing since the spring. There were two other model school districts in the city, one of which was involved in a serious disagreement over hiring practices with the teachers' union. All the teachers on the Du Pont Governing Board were members of the teachers' union. According to Paulman, all these teachers resigned from the governing board on orders from higher-ups in the union. A pretext was given that the chairman of the Du Pont Governing Board had met secretly with the chairmen of the other two governing boards without consulting the rest of the Du Pont Governing Board. Thus, when Mr. Weedman, the new district administrator, arrived in the summer he had a governing board made up solely of community residents.

A citywide school strike did occur during the fall of 1968. Although the local schools remained open, a considerable proportion of teachers struck. The strike was generally viewed in the neighborhood and in the city by many whites as being related to an attempt by blacks to take over control of the school system. This crisis thoroughly absorbed the governing board during the fall of 1968. Any innovations that it might have planned were impossible to institute.

In early 1969 the governing board, frustrated by its inability to bring about changes in the schools, focused its hostility on a principal of one school who was particularly uncooperative. This principal was Jewish and was ultimately fired. Unfortunately for the board, the parents' association in this particular school, comprised mainly of black, Puerto Rican, and Chinese women, supported the principal who had been fired even though the new principal was black. These women claimed that they were the community, and they had the right to control their own school. This issue was quickly picked up by elements of the community that had been hostile to PDP. They raised the claim that once again the schools were being controlled by a small faction to the exclusion of the broad community. By the summer of 1969 the community was split, with blacks, Puerto Ricans, and Chinese on both sides of the disagreement. In addition, a new governing board was due to be elected in the fall of 1969, and political factions were warring with one another in preparation for this election.

An interesting sidelight to this controversy developed when the original twenty teacher-assistants, who had been trained by Du Pont and ultimately placed in the schools in full-time positions, took the side of the union and the teachers in the school strike. According to Paulman, they began to mouth such statements as, "People don't really care about the schools" and "The teachers really are the ones who have the experience to run the schools." By and large they also remained hostile to the governing board.

One of the major factors that limited the effectiveness of the governing board was the vagueness of its authority. The citywide board of education did not adequately spell out what the board could and could not do. This failure engendered confusion and ultimately a great deal of cynicism. A major charge heard in the neighborhood about the governing board was that it had not been able to bring about any change in the local schools in two years. A review of the rewards and costs allocated through the governing board will illustrate further reasons for its ineffectiveness.

Rewards and costs of community control. The staff of an agency or an organization under community control is the major recipient of negotiable rewards offered by that organization. The primary reward received is money. It can be expected that the staff will attempt to ensure the continuation of such rewards and establish job security. However, when low-income people are hired for positions in an organization, they will be most concerned with job security since they do not have professional credentials and cannot easily get other jobs. Thus the teacher-assistants sided with the union against the governing board.

Once hired in local organizations, local people are almost impossible to fire without engaging in direct community conflict.[2] People recently poor will fight to maintain monetary rewards. There is a tendency for indigenous staffs to define themselves as "the community." Peers have great difficulty disciplining peers. The rhetoric of community control overlooks this fact.

Another strain involved in community control is the fact that once a group is authorized to control an institution, it has great difficulty in communicating its decisions back to the broad community. It tends to act without consulting the community—often because of a variety of constraints, such as time or political pressures. There are, in fact, few mechanisms whereby a group can adequately consult with the community. The local governing board has constantly been criticized for not consulting the community even though open public meetings have been held once every two weeks.[3] Unfortunately, these meetings have tended to become shouting matches. There has actually been no opportunity for mutual sharing of ideas and discussion as community conflict polarizes discussions.

The problems of adequately communicating with the community are grossly underestimated in the rhetoric of community control. Ultimately governing boards can become defined as "those people who are taking over." Removing board members becomes an extremely important emotional reward for those who have no way of influencing the board.

Another problem with the rhetoric of community control lies in its implication that involvement per se in community affairs is an extremely rewarding activity. In fact, the service rewards inherent in community participation are not that great and participation in general is not easily convertible for most people into ideological, negotiable, or emotional rewards. As one citizen deeply committed ideologically to community control reported, "This is not the greatest thing in the world. I would much rather be on the beach with my family."

This problem is especially severe if participation is restricted to decision-making. Only a rather limited number of people can actively participate in making decisions. *A sense of community or togetherness cannot be created in noncrisis situations solely by providing opportunities for decision-making.* In such situations, when opportunities for other types of participation are not available, alienation remains high as elites tend to take over. The formal structure and procedures of most organizations and institutions tend to single out such elites in low-income areas.[4] The strain toward limited participation of citizens ultimately cuts down on the possibility of the carrying out of a rational problem-solving process in which decisions are made dispassionately on full and extensive review of all the facts. In a situation of limited involvement of people, issues tend to be simplified into such areas as "power-grabbing" and "take-overs." (See page 187.)

A formalized view of administration and the functioning of bureaucracy is another oversimplification of the rhetoric of community control. Members of the governing board were constantly criticizing the district administrator for not immediately instituting policies and procedures that they had voted on. They failed to see why a principal could not be immediately fired. They were unable to grasp the concept that the bargaining, the trade-offs, the mutual expectations, and the obligations incurred over time are not easily tampered with. When policy changes are made, these mutual expectations are threatened and resistance can be expected. The rhetoric of community control overestimates the power of boards vis à vis an executive and the power of executives vis à vis staffs.[5] In the question of who controls whom, it is clear that both Hill and Paulman controlled Du Pont much more than the council controlled them.

Lastly, the rhetoric of community control overemphasizes power and control over policies and procedures to the exclusion of adequate consideration of the service or commodity produced by the institution or agency so controlled. Without some form of universal health insurance, community control of health services is not going to make a great deal of difference to the sick, especially the poor who are sick.

Some who advocate community control of local institutions, while admitting the above, often assume that once they are in control they can create a social movement to unite all poor, low-income communities in pressing for better and more adequate services.[6] More likely, as in the case of Du Pont, they will become the focus of community discontent because of the inadequacy of existing services and will be forced on the defensive to maintain their position of control. This problem will exist especially if local people hired to fill staff positions put job security before social action. Monetary rewards provided through jobs tend to inhibit the development of other types of rewards requisite for the formation of social movements. Major social problems cannot be solved primarily at the community level. The rhetoric of community control implies that they can.

The Reality of Community Control

What has been said in the previous section regarding community control is meant solely to point out the difficulties of instituting idealized versions of such a system. Given our country's democratic ethos, it is important that black, Puerto Rican, and Chinese citizens of Du Pont have the ability to influence local institutions. What is argued against is the naïve view of how people can obtain this influence. Without a procedure that ensures proportional representation of all segments of the community for the boards of local institutions both public and private, there is no real way that the community in toto can actually influence the functioning of local institutions. A most serious problem with the rhetoric of community control is that it implies that participation in the community is carried out solely by individuals in their status as citizens. In reality, as the Du Pont experience shows, participation is to a considerable extent affected by organizations and their interests. This is an important consideration. Note the following:

In Philadelphia, CAP boards were selected by direct elections, producing a phenomenon common to structureless politics—friends-and-neighbors voting patterns (the rate of voting for a candidate increases with the voters' geographical proximity to the candidate). The elections generated no base for members of the board that could hold them accountable. Consequently, members of the board were primarily concerned with divisible benefits—rewards for themselves and their friends and neighbors—rather than with the community more broadly conceived.

In New York, board members were selected at congresses of organizations. Members continued to be responsible to groups once they were in office and their power was enhanced because they were able to call upon the political resources of these groups as the occasion demanded. As compared with Philadelphia, the board members were concerned less about divisible benefits (although that element is always present) and more about issues affecting the welfare of the community as a whole. Thus less directly "democratic" procedures, in the sense of one-man-one-vote may be more "democratic" in their consequences, in the sense of spreading the benefits.[7]

At best, local institutions always tend to be controlled by certain segments more or less to the exclusion of others. The significant issues are the degree of control and its responsiveness to change. The old Du Pont Council really had attempted to control the neighborhood to the benefit of certain segments. Because it commanded relatively few resources, it operated in a slow, methodical, and devious pattern to develop its exchanges.

The new council has had many resources. It seeks even more in an aggressive, outspoken manner by demanding control of local institutions as a matter of right. Once such control is achieved, such organizations as the local governing board must decide whether they are primarily interested in promoting effective services such as quality education or in pyramiding their resources to gain control over other local institutions and building the groundwork for a social movement. The tactics and strategies required are different for each of these ends. To build a social movement an elite would have to maintain tight control over neighborhood institutions, operate to exclude those who threaten their control, and compromise on the quality of service if conflict should erupt, such as could occur by firing incompetents.

Community control has been espoused mainly by black or other nonwhite minority groups. Elements in these groups can be expected to push for the realization of this concept in slum areas where they make up a majority of the population.[8] Although Du Pont was clearly heterogeneous, it is likely that areas such as central Harlem in New York, comprised almost solely of blacks, are homogeneous only in race. Certain elements in such communities are certain to be more interested in effective service than in pyramiding resources for power. In time, conflict among factions and, to some extent, suppression of one group by another can be expected, just as occurred in Du Pont over the control and allocation of resources and rewards in the model school district.[9]

Malfunctioning public agencies and institutions make some form of local control necessary even if some conflict is bound to result. The important factor for social workers and others involved in such efforts is not to let the rhetoric obscure the reality. Although it is beyond the scope of this study to delineate the most appropriate form and manner of this control, it can be pointed out that without procedures and a structure planned to act as a counterweight, community control tends to become control of the community by some elements to the exclusion of others and does not necessarily lead to more effective services.[10]

On the basis of the Du Pont experience and the Poverty Program, it is clear that major social problems cannot be solved primarily from a neighborhood base, whether the solution is offered through services or through political organization.[11] This is the major reason that neighborhood councils have never spread throughout the country and the reason why community control will probably come to be seen as a useful, but not primary, means of attacking the social problems attendant on poverty.[12] Community involvement, citizen participation, and community control are not panaceas for all social ills.

A neighborhood is no more a small town than it is an underdeveloped country. The old Du Pont Council was successful primarily because it did not try to re-create an organic neighborhood. Rather it sought to relate the area to citywide systems. The extension of the council's current program emphasis to economic development and local taxation schemes unrelated to city and regional constraints in reality represents a return to the small-town ideology.

Ultimately, decisions about the extent and degree of control over services and functions accorded to localities must be made on the basis of evaluation of particular goals. Those who place "power to the people" above all other ends will not be much concerned with urban-ologists who raise questions about "who's minding the urban store," and vice versa. Those who are less ideological or technological will have to make judgments in particular service areas, such as health and education, about the value they will accord to such potential gains attributable to local control (diminution in red tape, innovation and responsiveness to local conditions, more effective accountability and lessening of citizen apathy, development and training of minority group leadership) as opposed to such potential losses (ineffective service results, obstructionism of citywide concerns, tyranny of the local major-ity over the local minority, and the overpoliticalization of human affairs). Undoubtedly, in most cases the answers will not be clear-cut. Judgments will have to be made about the amount of risk worth taking to achieve desired ends. Yet, even evolutionary social change cannot be achieved without risks.

The purpose in this study of looking behind the mask of democratic mythology has been to show that risks and gains, rewards and costs, are part of life and not to be treated as the unfortunate, illegitimate by-products of democratic processes. Ideals and mythology shape our lives and should not be discarded lightly. There is a danger in simply destroying myths that no longer completely suit reality without provid-ing a more appropriate set of ideals. The democratic ideal has great vibrancy. Whatever adaptations must be made in it in the coming decades can only be enhanced by a clear view of how it operates.

Summary

In Du Pont the council seems to have lost its identity; other orga-nizations are at the center of community life. A new outbreak of racial violence would surely expose the weakness of the present structure of the council. It is difficult to maintain all elements of a heterogeneous community in one organization. Since there was not enough leadership available outside of the council and unidentified with it, it was perhaps inevitable that, once the Poverty Program came into being, the council would become the means for forceful furthering of the interests of nonwhites.

When the urban renewal project is completed in 1972, a preponderance of middle-income whites will be moving into the community. At that time new resources will be available for community affairs. It is likely that this group will find the council a congenial organizational form through which to make its impact on the community. It is also likely that disputes among and between nonwhite groups may make the council valuable again as the arm of a new coalition.

The past history of the Du Pont Council should be of value to this coalition in setting its goals. The real value of neighborhood councils lies in making institutions and agencies, public and private, responsive to the needs of the local citizenry, in addition to ameliorating local problems such as racial conflicts. This responsiveness does not necessarily require complete decentralization and community control of vital services. The important question in large urban areas is what decisions should be left to local decision-making, what services should be decentralized, and what degree of community control and citizen participation should be encouraged.[13]

More local control than generally exists now is in order. The answer to the question of how much is necessary rests on judgments of the best way to achieve efficiency of services while at the same time to decrease feelings of alienation and powerlessness on the part of the citizenry. The answers are clearly not entirely local in nature or design. Experimentation with a variety of arrangements is vital, for it is likely that different combinations and types of citizen participation and control will be needed to suit the varied conditions that exist in urban areas. Overseeing such experimentation is an important function for neighborhood councils.

The early part of the century saw the development of such concepts as the city manager, nonpartisan elections, and the extension of civil service. Civic reformers assumed then that these reforms would maximize rewards to all segments of the population. The difficulties of achieving such an end are clear. At this point in time a new wave of reform is beginning. Those who would ride this wave would do well to balance themselves on the algebra of rewards and costs in urban life.

NOTES

1. See, for example, Daniel M. Fox, "Community Corporations: Problems and Prospects" (Paper delivered at the National Conference on Social Welfare, New York City, May 27, 1969.)

2. When their jobs are threatened, indigenous staffs are able to call into play personal contacts and friendships that they have built up over the years in the community.

3. The same problem has occurred in community corporations elected by the poor citizens of poverty areas. See Steven Leeds, "The Lower East Side Poverty Election," mimeographed (New York: Columbia University School of Social Work Research Center, 1967).

4. Another factor that affects the degree and quality of citizen participation is the way in which community control over local institutions comes about. Conflict over this issue can be expected to activate somewhat different groups of people than would be activated in a routine, calm situation.

5. For a discussion of the desire for professionalism on the part of teachers and how this limits community control, see Arthur F. Salz, "Policymaking Under Decentralization," *The Urban Review*, III (June 1969), 25, 31–33.

6. For a discussion of this strategy and the results achieved by it in the Poverty Program, see Harold H. Weissman, "Social Action in a Social Work Context," *Community Development in the Mobilization For Youth Experience*, ed. Harold H. Weissman (New York: Association Press, 1969).

7. *Citizen Involvement In Urban Affairs*, HUD-NYU Summer Study (New York: New York University, 1968), p. 80–81.

8. One reason is, as the Du Pont experience shows, that ethnically determined rewards are still highly salient. Community control as currently espoused because of its explicitness and formality makes accommodation in the short run less likely and intergroup conflict more likely. In the past the intransigence of white groups to exchanges with nonwhite groups to a great extent has forced this formal strategy.

9. James Madison was one of the first to argue clearly against the direct democracy of the small town or community control. He feared that in such situations a majority would tyrannize a minority since a grass-roots ideology had no expectation of serious division within its constituency and consequently no provision for the protection of the minority. See Robert C. Wood, "A Reexamination of Local Democracy," *Democracy in Urban America*, ed. O. P. Williams and C. Press (Chicago: Rand McNally & Co., 1961), p. 120.

10. The danger that the vociferous few will gain control over schools can be countered by election processes that ensure sufficient time to inform parents, ensure forms of proportional representation, mandate public reports, etc. Bertram Beck suggests six ways of ensuring effective service and community control over the provision of services by local institutions: board membership, hiring local citizens for staff positions, organizing client-consumer groups, providing legal services for clients, an ombudsman, and providing a choice among services for clients. "Can Agency and Client Be Coequals in Policy-Making and Administration?" (Paper presented at the National Conference on Social Welfare, New York City, May 27, 1969).

11. For a discussion of this point, see Frances Fox Piven, "Community Control: Beyond the Rhetoric," *New Generation*, L (Fall 1968), 7–10. David K. Cohen in "The Price of Community Control," *Commentary*, XLVIII (July 1069), 23–32, suggests that temporary political peace between the races can be bought through community control although not necessarily changing the social and economic inequalities that exist.

12. For a comprehensive review of all the issues related to community control, see *Citizen Involvement In Urban Affairs*. One of the important latent functions of the drive for community control is that it may force city-wide political groups to more fully open themselves up to black participation. Piven, "Community Control," is not sanguine about this possibility.
13. For a discussion of this question, see Daniel Bell and Virginia Held, "The Community Revolution," *The Public Interest*, XVI (Summer 1969). For an exposition of the case for viewing a neighborhood as an autonomous political entity, see Milton Kotler, *Neighborhood Governments: The Local Foundations of Political Life* (New York: Bobbs-Merrill, 1969).

Appendices
Bibliography
Index

A Summary of the Utility
of an Exchange Model
for Community
Organization Practice

This study was motivated by two primary convictions: (1) the time and the effort that citizens make available for community improvement are precious resources that a community must utilize as efficiently and effectively as possible, and (2) the community organizer is an equally valuable resource; the more able he is in carrying out his task, the better the community will be.

The major intent of this study has been to explore how exchanges take place in neighborhood councils and how an awareness of these exchanges can be utilized by community organizers to carry out their work more effectively. No claim is made that this awareness of exchanges will solve all a worker's problems. Nor can Du Pont's relative success in performing many functions be taken as proof that a council that operates in a similar fashion can in every neighborhood perform the same functions. Actually, the transposition of a packaged council into neighborhoods of varying makeups would be unrealistic since a single structure or set of procedures cannot fit every situation.

Du Pont's success was related to its ability to adapt structures, select goals, and modify procedures to the conditions that existed in its neighborhood. For other councils to achieve similar success, they would need operable guidelines on which to base decisions about structure, goals, and procedures. In order for such guidelines to be developed, this study has applied an exchange model to the problems of the functioning of neighborhood councils.

182					APPENDIX A

Recommendations from the Study of Du Pont

Study of the Neighborhood

A common error made in the HEED councils was the assumption that the rewards sought by local people could be neatly categorized under such headings as health, housing, recreation, and education. In actuality, the rewards that people sought were much more diverse, and they often sought these rewards not as individuals, but as members of groups and organizations. Ethnic groups in Du Pont desired certain rewards for themselves; the political clubs desired other rewards, as did the Protestant missions and the parents' associations. In addition, the salient rewards were often just as likely to be of an emotional nature as they were to be related to the provision of services. The convertibility of council activities into emotional rewards is always a vital factor.

The rewards sought from a neighborhood organization by the ethnic subsystems in Du Pont bear repeating. In great measure these rewards account for the participation in the council or lack thereof of members of these groups. The Jews sought an organization that would guarantee their physical safety and provide a high quality of community services. The white Protestants sought an organization that would ensure good government and would dislodge the neighborhood from the control of ethnic politicians. The Puerto Ricans sought an organization that would unite them. The Italians sought an organization that would maintain their internal solidarity and their control of the neighborhood. The Negroes sought an organization that would accept them as equal participants. The Chinese sought an organization that would provide services for them as consumers but not as participants. The rewards that Du Pont offered were not equally salient to all subsystems in the neighborhood. Part of the reason was that offering a salient reward to one implied a consequent cost to another. Participation in and antagonism to the council can be related to the fact that Du Pont provided certain subsystems with more rewards than others and, in like measure, imposed more costs on certain subsystems than others.

Even though a worker has a thorough knowledge of the potentially salient rewards for groups in a neighborhood, he cannot assume that citizens wish to join a neighborhood council to attain these rewards. There may be already existing, even though ineffective, means for people to secure them. A worker must, therefore, have knowledge of the most favorable conditions under which a neighborhood council can be set up.

The availability of surplus resources, such as time, money, and facilities, is the key to the formation of organizations. From Du Pont's experience it can be expected that this condition will occur under two sets of circumstances—a crisis and/or a coalition—or some combination of both. Should these conditions not inhere in a neighborhood, greater difficulty can be expected. Regardless, whatever the situation, a worker must assess which people and groups in the neighborhood possess the required resources for building an organization and what they want in exchange for these resources. This assessment should alert a worker to the organization's potential friends and antagonists. Of these, other organizations are of prime importance.

Selecting a Structure

Councils err when they immediately form committees, elect officers, and write constitutions without considering the effects of such actions.[1] Du Pont's structure tended to recruit those with middle-class skills and attributes. Its structure was set at an early stage due to the pattern of exchanges that developed from its efforts to deal with the crisis of gang warfare. Its domination from the outset by social workers and Protestant ministers, who devised its formal manner of operation, determined that lower- and working-class people, with different interests and modes of participating, would not likely view the council as a rewarding organization.

If a crisis brings a council into being, the crisis must be dealt with so that the exchanges made in the course of its efforts to resolve the crisis do not undermine the council's future. It must be emphasized that the way in which a council enters into exchanges early in its existence greatly affects its chances of survival. Consequently, a worker must be aware of the conflicts of interest that exist within a neighborhood. Since in most neighborhoods there will be stratification and conflicts of interest, a council must decide the degree that it wishes to promote one interest over another. In Du Pont the coalition made a clear choice—the Negroes and Puerto Ricans over the Italians. A determination of a council's real goals, and the location of the resources it will need to attain these, will help a worker select a structure. Such a determination may, for example, rule out a council made up of all local organizations and groups.

Some structures are better suited than others for recruiting the desired resources because they offer more rewards and less costs. A mass citizens' organization is more likely than a neighborhood council to recruit the resources of low-income people since its structure is geared to the kinds of programs and activities in which their resources can be utilized. As illustrated by Du Pont, a neighborhood council operating through a formal, hierarchical arrangement of committees tends to appeal to the middle class.

A neighborhood organization can take many forms: a council made up of citizens and organizational representatives, a series of block organizations represented in an overall council, a mass citizens' organization, ad hoc organizations set up to deal with specific problems, a set of advisory groups to local agencies and departments, or a combination of any or all of these. The Du Pont experience also indicates that sometimes more than one type of organization is needed for a council to function effectively. For example, Du Pont was unofficially responsible for the formation of the insurgent political clubs. Whatever the structure or structures chosen, they must be suited to the recruitment of the resources needed to attain goals.

Traditionally, an accepted principle of neighborhood councils has been that everyone in a neighborhood should be involved. The Du Pont experience underscores how difficult it is to do this in one organization. Such an organization tends to develop an image that defines itself as rewarding to some, nonrewarding to others. Sridharan points to selective recruitment as a major factor in the success of a stable St. Louis council that he investigated.[2] Similarly, Du Pont knew that it had to recruit working-class Italians, and did so by providing a structure for them where they could receive a range of rewards in exchange for their resources.

Selecting and Attaining Goals

Paradoxically, one of the worst errors a council can make is to select projects based simply on the presumption that they are good for the neighborhood.[3] There are many worthwhile projects. Some are accomplishable, some are not. Some may tend to weaken a council, others to enhance it.

Although goal selection ultimately is based on the values and interests of participants, it must also be based on an overall plan of action. By understanding the exchanges that are developed through any one project, it is possible to relate what has been exchanged to other projects in the same area, for example, the UNICEF carnival helped develop a coalition of parents' associations, which secured a replacement for PS 4. Linking systems, pyramiding resources, imposing costs for nonparticipation, and lowering costs for participation are some of the techniques that are useful in developing a council's exchange potential and overall plan of action to attain goals.

The major utility of an exchange model is that it offers a way of securing resources other than simply recruiting participants possessing resources on the basis of their interest in projects. It suggests that if a council does not have the rewards to exchange for resources it needs, it must select projects and carry them out in ways that will develop its reward supply or exchange system. The choice of project goals is, therefore, the most crucial decision a council can make. Du Pont's survival rested on its ability to select projects like the Little League that offered the kinds of rewards that could bridge the conflicts of interest in the neighborhood.

Resources, as noted, can be recruited for one project, which, upon completion, can supply more resources to be used in exchange for others that can be used for another project. A council thus need not be limited to procedures or projects commensurate with the resources immediately available; nor in recruiting participants is it forced to rely on the rewards intrinsically related to the project under consideration. This concept is extremely important in view of the fact that those who possess the resources to carry out a project often do not wish to participate. A wide range of procedures is open to an organization: committee meetings, informal discussions, mass meetings, parades, boycotts, forums, delegations, surveys, acts of civil disobedience, clinics, etc. Staff workers must consider the kind of resources required to carry out any procedure. Exclusive reliance on any one procedure may exclude from the organization those whose participation is needed, but who do not have the required resources for carrying out the procedure.

In setting up procedures or any other aspect of council functioning, the costs of participation must be considered. The rewards that a council offers must outweigh the costs of participation. The true value of a potential reward cannot be gauged without considering costs. A major dilemma of neighborhood organizations—that of getting people to participate and invest their resources when projects per se are of limited saliency—can be dealt with by gauging the costs as well as the rewards of participation to people and organizations in their multiple statuses and interrelationships. Most of Du Pont's active participants were able to get from council participation rewards that were useful to them in other systems outside of the council in which they participated, for they did not disregard their desire for rewards beyond those specifically related to council projects. Active participation in Du Pont was related to a participant's ability to maximize rewards in many statuses. The opportunity ladders that Du Pont developed were useful for recruiting upwardly mobile members. Likewise, the opportunity for organizations to receive rewards useful for the attainment of their noncouncil goals was extremely important in maintaining their cooperation.

Council Stability and Leadership

Since one cause of instability is a lack of reward-producing projects, the search for new projects during periods of instability is not promising. Another, even more important cause is the lack of diffuse sources of commitment. The binding exchanges inherent in such commitment may be developed through ceremonial events and meetings, organizational symbols, expressive functions, and patterns of socialization. Stability may be further enhanced by maintaining internal consensus through segregating dissident groups so that each can maximize its rewards.

A major function of leadership in Du Pont was to secure the resources needed to attain its goals. If leadership cannot perform this function, then, as Dennis has suggested, it must be replaced if a council is to survive. General organizational skills and personality traits should not be used as the criteria for electing a chairman. A new organization would be well advised to select leaders in terms of their ability to control or develop a pool of needed resources. In Du Pont this ability was, in great measure, related to membership in a particular ethnic group, organizational affiliation, and political contacts.

The Worker

The pattern of a staff worker who is paid from funds secured from nonlocal sources and is working with local organizations is a familiar one in the poverty programs around the country. In all probability these workers face problems similar to those faced by Hill. Given the fact that they inevitably become the center of communication in their organizations, have the most power, and are constrained to prod and backstop members, such workers must devise ways of shifting to the membership the control of their organizations if the organizations are to be independent and self-sustaining.

The field of community organization has in recent years moved away from a single-role model for a worker. Rothman has defined eight interventive roles based on different combinations of directiveness and immediate empirical goal categories. He suggests that a worker must diagnostically draw upon these roles dependent upon the community problem and situation.[4] What a worker needs is the skill to make a situational analysis that will lead him to choose the proper procedures and techniques. Rothman's paper stops short of specifying how this situational analysis may be made.

The Du Pont experience offers some guidelines. First, the centrality of the worker's leadership and power must be accepted, not as an unfortunate consequence of the inability of the membership to perform organizational functions, but as a needed requisite for the worker to develop a viable organization. Secondly, the worker must realize the distinction between solving neighborhood problems and building an organization capable of solving neighborhood problems. He must be concerned with building lasting commitment and solidarity. Von Hoffman notes: "The organizer's first job is to organize, not right wrongs, not avenge injustice, not to win the battle for freedom. That is the task of people who will accomplish it through the organization if it ever gets built. When things are looked at through the glass of organizational calculation, they assume new shapes."[5]

Thirdly, in Von Hoffman's terms, the worker must "calculate" the effect of various projects and procedures on neighborhood groups whose resources are required to achieve the organization's ends. (Du Pont made such calculations with the Little League.) The worker must develop the supply of rewards and the image of the organization. The more clearly these are developed the more likely the organization is to be under the control of those who seek such rewards. And lastly, the worker must accept and plan for two different types of participation. He must ensure that leadership commensurate with organizational tasks can come forward. He must also ensure that there are meaningful organizational tasks for those who do not wish to assume the responsibility of leadership. Von Hoffman states the following caveat: "At the beginning to keep the organization very loose, spread the responsibilities and the conspicuous places around. This permits you and the new membership, which you are supposed to be recruiting, to judge the talent, and it keeps things sufficiently porous so that new talent isn't blocked off."[6]

Utility of the Model

The choice of rewards as one of the central concepts of this study was based on the contention that this concept is more operable than the more traditional one of needs. The concept of rewards implies a dynamic: something is done and as a reward something is granted. It suggests a way of understanding organizational behavior as a form of exchange. The concept of need does not have this dynamic implication. If anything, it leads to thinking solely about how an organization like a council can meet needs, without consideration of the costs to participants inherent in what is done to meet needs. Workers must be able to take into account such considerations.

The purpose of explicating the exchange model has not been to develop Machiavellian community organizers. Rather it has been to show that exchanges that occur in human and organizational interaction significantly affect community affairs and that ideals such as participatory democracy cannot be attained simply through the use of democratic forms, procedures, and exhortations.

As noted in the Epilogue, the community cannot really control local institutions if the only opportunities provided are those for participation in decision-making at public meetings. An elite will in such instances ultimately gain control. The structuring of participation is necessary to ensure the interest and awareness of large numbers of people, most of whom may only be interested, for example, in writing a newspaper column or in tutoring, but who through their participation gain information and knowledge, which in and of itself is valuable in a democracy. Ultimately, if these people so choose, they are able to move on to decision-making.

People wish to be needed and rewarded for fulfilling their obligations. What must be recognized is that only a rather small finite number of people can actually participate in organizational decision-making. In the Du Pont Council there just were not sufficient activities that people felt were important and that they could do something about. English researchers speaking of how civil emergencies were met in wartime England offer a clue to the reason for such a situation. They note that "people talk of the war as one of the most enjoyable periods of their life."[7] In noncrisis situations a variety of opportunities for rewarding participation must be carefully planned. In the long run these opportunities are diminished in importance and value by the presence of paid staff who can actually do most of what needs to be done.

Opportunities, such as were provided by the Little League, are needed in urban society for people from different groups and strata to get to know one another informally. Formal meetings do not adequately serve this purpose, especially since one of the purposes of people's getting to know one another informally is to make it easier for them to come to formal agreements.

Decentralization of community services alone or accompanied by community control will not necessarily lead to more effective services or a heightened sense of community. Overseeing the needed experimentation in such methods of service delivery is an important function for neighborhood councils.

Summary

Hill and his HEED colleagues had two major concerns: are councils useful mechanisms to change neighborhoods; and, if so, what could they, as workers, do to make them more effective? This study has explored with a view to these concerns the exchanges that occurred in a relatively successful council. It remains for future community organizers to test the usefulness of the recommendations that have been made.

Although it is clear that councils in and of themselves are not a solution to pressing social problems, one of the best answers to those who question the utility of neighborhood councils was pointedly made at a HEED conference attended by leading community figures. After some discussion and a listing of Du Pont's and other councils' accomplishments, a local politician pointed across the table to a powerful city politician and said: "Well, this man can do everything you say neighborhood councils have done simply by lifting his telephone off its hook. What do we need neighborhood councils for?" The chairman of Du Pont leaned forward and replied: "Well, then, why didn't he?"

NOTES

1. They also err when they choose the classic structure and assume that the interests of all groups are such that they can immediately work together in one organization.
2. K. V. Sridharan, "Area Approach to Social Welfare Planning," (Ph.D. diss. Ohio State University, 1959), p. 67.
3. Another common error is to select only those goals which reflect total neighborhood concerns, e.g., education and crime. Often a council would be well served to select goals of primary concern to one group, e.g., to get the Puerto Ricans a place to meet. If Du Pont had done this, it would probably have had greater Puerto Rican participation.
4. Jack Rothman, "Goals and Roles in Community Organization," *Social Work,* IX (April 1964), 29.
5. Nicholas Von Hoffman, "Finding and Making Leaders," mimeographed (New York: Congress of Racial Equality, n.d.), p. 8. This paper contains a detailed analysis of many practice problems that confront community organizers.
6. Ibid., p. 4.
7. Richard Hauser and Elizabeth Hauser, *The Fraternal Society* (New York: Random House, 1963), p. 54.

Schedule for Interviewing
Council Participants

[This schedule was used as a guide for the researchers as they interviewed each member of the council. Interviews were held between October 1, 1963, and June 1, 1964.]

I'd like to ask you some questions about _____ council and your participation in it. First:

A.   How did you become involved with the council? When did you join?

B.   Did you ever receive a written or mimeographed invitation, or read a newspaper notice inviting you to join the council? Did you respond to this invitation?

C.   Do you represent another organization in the council? If so, describe its purpose. What position do you hold? In which ways has or could the council help your organization?

D.   Were you or your organization reluctant to join for any reason?

E.*   How does your organization hear about what the council is doing? Do you make periodic reports?

* To be answered only if participant is representing an organization.

F.*   Do you encourage the members of your home organization to join or attend council meetings? If not, why not?

G.*   Has your group ever been in conflict or competition in any way with the council?

H.   When you cannot attend a council meeting for some reason, how do you find out what has happened at the meeting? Do you send a representative from your organization?

I.   To what other organizations do you belong (*for example*, PTA, church or political groups, business clubs, labor unions, fraternities, or lodges)? Name them.

J.   Describe your participation in them (positions held, degree of interest, activities).

K.   People often join organizations for certain reasons but remain active for other reasons. Does this apply to you in relation to the council? What do you enjoy doing most?

L.   Do you see any council members outside of the council? In what situation?

M.   Do you think the council itself should have more social activities and programs?

N.   Do you think the council should continue meeting during the summer?

* To be answered only if participant is representing an organization.

O.   What do you see as your contribution to the council?

P.   What should the council do?

Q.   Rate the importance of the following areas in terms of your own life
     at this moment?

     If you had problems in any of these areas, would you join with others
     in the council to try and solve them? (Give slip to participant.)

     Yes   No
     _____   _____   Teen-age behavior
     _____   _____   Pleasant living conditions
     _____   _____   Family relationships: wife, husband, children
     _____   _____   A good job
     _____   _____   Good relationships with other racial and religious
                        groups
     _____   _____   Good school facilities and institutions
     _____   _____   Personal or family health
     _____   _____   Opportunities to make friends
     _____   _____   Parks and recreational facilities for children and adults
     _____   _____   Others

R.   How did the community deal with problems before the council was
     formed?

S.   If you had to decide which project the council should work on, which
     would you place first, second, etc.?

     _____ Organizing social functions   _____ Tenant-landlord problems
     _____ Better credit facilities   _____ Family-living course
     _____ More recreational and   _____ Improving schools
            park facilities   _____ Honesty of storekeepers
     _____ Better employment   _____ Improving health facilities
            opportunities   _____ Interracial relations
     _____ Delinquency

T.   What are the main accomplishments of the council?

U.   What, if anything, do you think is wrong with the council? How could it be improved?

V.   Would you say that there are any conflicts between members or groups in the council? How are they resolved?

W.   What can the council do to insure that individual members will go along with council decisions?

X.   Why do some people drop out of the council?

Y.   Which groups of people who are not members would strengthen the council if they joined? Have they ever been contacted? Why do you think they haven't joined?

Z.   Are there (or have there been) occasions when the council shies away from certain problem areas because of fear of or actual repercussions in the neighborhood?

A.A.   Are there any people other than the chairman and the worker whom you would really call a leader in the council? Give names.

B.B.   Why do you think the leaders work as hard as they do? (Probe for specific people.)

C.C. What qualities make for a good chairman? (Probe areas of education, organizational experience, occupation.)

Now let's talk a little about the worker and the council:

D.D. What do you think the worker should do? Do you really think a professional worker is necessary? If you had forty hours a week to devote to the council, would you accomplish as much as the worker?

E.E. Are there things he or she should not do? What about minute-writing, phone reminders, etc.? What do you think about _____ and the way he's done his job?

F.F. Does it ever happen that the council goes along with the worker rather than disagree or come into conflict? What do you think would occur to the council if the worker were withdrawn and not replaced?

G.G. Do you read the *Du Pont News* regularly, have you watched or heard about the Du Pont sports parade? Have you participated in any function other than meetings?

To sum up:

H.H. As a result of your membership, what have you learned or how have you been affected?

I.I. Are there things which we did not cover which you feel would be important for us to know about the council?

Now I'd like to get your general opinions about a few things:

J.J.   Suppose some outstanding young man asked your advice on what would be one of the best areas of work to aim toward. Which one would you think you would advise him to aim toward?

_____ Outdoor work
_____ Clerical work
_____ Craft work—plumber, carpenter, mechanic
_____ Service work—domestic, restaurant, hotel
_____ Work with people—minister, social worker, teacher
_____ Business

K.K.   Now I'd like to tell you a little story and get your opinion on it. Suppose some young man from this neighborhood asked your advice on whether he should take a new job or not. The new job, he tells you, means that he will have to see much less of his parents and neighborhood friends. On the other hand, he feels that the new job offers him a chance to have a new way of life and respectability. The new job pays the same as the one he has now. What would you advise him to do?

1. Keep his old job and thereby keep his ties to his parents and neighborhood friends
2. Take the new job offering him a new way of life and respectability
3. D.K. [don't know]
4. N.A. [no answer]

L.L.   About how much schooling do you think most young men need these days to get along well in the world?

0. Eight years or less (grammar school)
1. Some high school
2. High school graduation
3. Some college
4. College graduation (four years of college)
5. More than four years of college
6. High school graduation plus noncollege technical training
7. D.K.

M.M. Do you think most successful people were able to get ahead because of their ability, hard work, luck, or pull? (If more than one answer is given, ask the respondent, "Which is more important?")

    1. Ability
    2. Hard work
    3. Luck
    4. Pull
    5. Other
    6. D.K.

N.N. Which one of the following jobs would you be most likely to take if you had the chance?

    1. A poor-paying job that is secure
    2. A job with good pay, but with a fifty-fifty chance of losing it
    3. A job with high pay, but with a great risk of losing it
    4. D.K.

Name_____ Sex_____ Age_____

Address_____ Marital Status_____

Race_____ Religion_____

Family Income: _____ Under $2,000
              _____ $2,000 – 3,500
              _____ 3,500 – 4,500
              _____ 4,500 – 6,000
              _____ 6,000 – 7,500
              _____ Over   7,500

Occupation of both husband and wife: _____

_____

Years of school completed _____

Number of children _____

Date_____ Interviewer_____ Place_____

Outline for
Field Observations

I. Problem-Solving

A. What is the problem? Who initiated it?
B. How and on what bases was the decision made to work on this problem?
C. What are the required resources? Where are they located?
D. Are sufficient resources available? What inducements are to be used to secure the needed resources?
E. What action was taken? Was there consensus or conflict?
F. What rewards and sanctions are people who work on this problem deriving? How are rewards distributed?
G. How and by what mechanisms was the activity around this problem translated into solidarity or commitment?
H. Which part or parts of the problem were solved? Why? Why were others unsolved?
I. How will the activities of the council in relation to this problem affect the neighborhood?

II. Meeting Analysis

A. What rewards were available to individuals and organizations? Note mechanisms of allocation and coordination.
B. What sanctions were meted out? By whom?
C. What functions did expressive activities play at this meeting?
D. Was there tension or conflict at this meeting? How was it resolved?

E. What communication occurred about noncouncil activities?

F. Describe the participation of members (roles filled, rewards sought)?

G. Who did not actively participate?

H. Who seemed to exercise power? On what was the power based?

I. On what bases did the council seek to legitimize its activities?

J. To what extent did learning of any kind take place?

K. What systemic needs of the council were articulated at this meeting?

L. What did new members do at this meeting?

Worker's Log

Council_____ Worker_____ Date_____

Administrative tasks:

Contacts with members and others (I, T. O*):

Purpose and outcome:

* The letter *I* refers to worker-originated contacts. *T* refers to contacts originated by others. *O* refers to any other type of contact.

Research Procedures

At the beginning of this study, in September of 1962, HEED comprised four councils. One of these four was eliminated from consideration because of an earlier focus on group therapy and the continued presence of members whose actions were considered too atypical to allow the council to be used for comparative purposes. Another council was eliminated because of a confused staff picture and a lack of demographic and survey data for the area. Du Pont immediately seemed a logical choice because of its longevity and well-documented success. SECA offered the possibility of watching the birth of a council.

Timing and Sources of Data

The first two months of the study were used to develop and check methods of observing and recording data. A system of recording was developed whereby each council activity could be followed in chronological sequence from inception to conclusion, that is, each week the discussions about the sports parade were recorded on separate index cards so that a complete record of this event was available. In addition, cards were kept for each meeting on such organizational phenomena as socialization patterns, imposition of sanctions, and distribution of rewards. At the end of this trial period, the strategy of the study was set: all activities of Du Pont and SECA from approximately November 1, 1962, through October 1, 1963, would be observed and recorded following the aforementioned procedures. The summer of 1963 would be used for preliminary analyses of the data, for pretesting the questionnaire to be administered orally at interviews with all council participants, and for a demographic, historical, organizational, and ethnic study of the neighborhood. For the first year the research staff included the project director and an assistant. Later part-time interviewers were utilized.

In the main, this strategy was carried out. However, due to changes in staff, internal conflict, and general demoralization of its membership, SECA never developed as an organization and remained skeletal in nature. Observations were discontinued in the spring of 1963. Interviews of Du Pont participants as well as nonparticipants began on October 1, 1963, and continued until June 1, 1964. Of the 125 participants in 1962–1963, 88 were interviewed. Ten moved from the area, 2 were incapacitated by illness and unable to be interviewed, 5 refused, 7 repeatedly broke appointments, and 13 could not be contacted for various reasons.

Observations of Du Pont continued on a selective basis through June of 1964. From January 1, 1963, to September 1, 1963, the project director attended HEED staff meetings as well as board and executive committee meetings. Weekly discussions were also held with Hill to study his log of activities between meetings, ·which he kept from January to May of 1963.

Other sources of data included census tract material, voluminous past records of Du Pont's activities, Mobilization for Youth surveys, and interviews with influential nonparticipants in the Du Pont neighborhood, as well as interviews with selected former members who had once been active. Thirty-four such interviews were held. In addition, a major source of data was the constant informal discussions that occurred between the researcher and members and staff alike.

Procedures for Open-Ended Questions

Individual codes were developed for open-ended questions in the "Schedule for Interviewing Council Participants" (see Appendix B). They were based upon the questions' objectives, analysis of a sample of responses, and the frequency of particular kinds of answers. In carrying out this procedure, each verbatim response was read and assigned a code or codes. Since ideas, not words, were coded, the exact phrase listed in the codes may not have appeared in the answer. The idea behind the words was sought, not just the words. A miscellaneous code was used for all genuine ideas not contained in the code proper because of infrequent occurrence. In the one question, where members' responses were not used as the basis for developing the codes, the actual coding of responses was done by two coders as a check on reliability. In general coding procedures were followed as outlined in *Codebook, Adult Survey* of the Mobilization for Youth.

The Relationship of the Observer and the Observed

As others have noted, the classic, disinterested, objective, passive stance of a scientific observer is difficult to maintain in a participant-observation study. Neither the Du Pont staff nor the members wanted simply to be observed. To be asked constantly to give in a relationship, receiving nothing in return, is a situation that most people resist. With the staff this problem was handled to a certain extent by giving periodic progress reports on the course of the study, which designated when interviews would begin, when pretesting of the questionnaire would take place, etc. In addition each HEED staff member was asked, partially as a means of involvement, to prepare a set of questions that he hoped the study would answer, to complete time studies of his job, and to describe his frustrations and satisfaction with the work.

Two vital factors had to be dealt with to gain the cooperation of the total HEED staff. The first was the assurance that the researchers would not violate the confidence of the agency, especially in relation to the agency that employed the researchers. Every effort was made not to become a communication link between the two agencies since considerable friction already existed between them on topics other than research. This decision was carried to the point of not discussing the study with the researchers' colleagues who had no official connection with the study, and gave the project a semisecret aura. When word of this secrecy filtered back to the HEED staff, there was considerable joking about the study and a generally more positive feeling toward it. When one of the researchers made a verbal slip to the effect that he worked for HEED, it was clear to all that at least there was no spy in their midst.

The other crucial factor was the need to impress upon the staff that the study would not be used to evaluate their work. Formal presentations emphasized this point. In many informal discussions with workers about the study, the point was made that the research was concerned with their position in the councils and the knowledge available in the field of community organization, rather than their particular strengths and weaknesses as workers. The mere fact of the researchers' presence, plus the evident fact as time passed that they were not communication links to the workers' supervisor, tended to make the researchers the workers' confidants. Hill and the project director often grumbled together about such problems as the number of meetings each week and the late hours, the grouchiness of certain people, and the problems of being a social worker. If anything, staff workers came to welcome the researchers' presence. The project director was always invited to HEED staff parties and informal get-togethers.

The problem of gaining the confidence of the membership was considerably more complicated. HEED's staff workers were few in number and professionally committed to research and the advancement of knowledge; the membership was not. An initial error made by the researchers in Du Pont was entering the council via the general meeting. A brief presentation at each of the committee meetings would have been much more helpful. Even there, the pattern of attendance was so varied that only a repetition at three or four consecutive meetings would have served to introduce the study to all concerned. In Du Pont the question, "Why was the council so successful?" was an easy selling point. However, in SECA the membership was so changing and confusion about the council so endemic that very few people came to understand the nature of the research. Most people simply identified the researchers with the agency to which they were attached, although in the main this agency was not associated with its research function.

Fortunately the chairman of the Du Pont Council was interested in the research idea and served to legitimize the study. Of greatest importance he was well-liked and had considerable influence in the council. Nevertheless, such questions as "How did we do today?" and "Did you give us a good report?" bore witness to the existence of confusion and anxiety about the researchers' presence.

The main problem was encountered in the sports committee. The researchers were unprepared for the initial reaction of this committee, which at the time was engaged in a secessionist movement from the council and an open vendetta against the researchers' sponsoring agency. Instead of a pleasant reception, there was real hostility. The working-class pattern of this group was in sharp contrast to the polite middle-class ways of the rest of the council. At one point the committee voted the research assistant out until his agency made a donation to its program. At the next meeting the project director made a speech describing the purposes of the study and its ultimate value to sports in this and other neighborhoods. The research assistant suggested the use of the phrase "writing a book" instead of "conducting a study." There was a noticeable change in the atmosphere of the group when some of the members realized that they might be written up in a book. Enough votes were changed so that the researchers were allowed to remain.

Some of the sports committee members were never more than polite. Others who were initially hostile became friendly and responsive. The hostility, rivalry, and suspicion that existed within the committee made friendliness with everyone difficult; it became necessary for the researchers to be selective about whom they sat next to at meetings, as well as with whom they entered and left meetings. This held true at meetings of all committees. The problem was not always easy to handle since after a time personal preferences intervened.

The chairman of the council often used the presence of the researchers as a source of humor. He would ask the researchers if they had nominations or if everything met with their approval. New people at meetings were momentarily puzzled at the laughter that followed these remarks. These comments served to highlight the researchers' role and introduced the researchers to many new people in a most favorable way. They also served to reduce the tension and anxiety that might have been caused by the researchers' presence. In this case the observer was giving something to the group in exchange for what he took. Using the exchange conception, it can be hypothesized that the amount of information received by the observers was in part related to the costs that individuals and the group incurred and the rewards that they received from the observers' presence.

Initial Formulations

Some mention deserves to be made about procedures other than observational techniques. The study did not proceed from a well-formulated model of a neighborhood council or voluntary organization. It began first with a series of practice questions about neighborhood councils, which were then formulated into hypotheses based on knowledge of organizational functioning derived from other studies. These hypotheses were checked against the possibility of securing data to verify them. This step resulted in considerable refining of the hypotheses.

The hypotheses at this point were disconnected and unrelated to one another. By placing them in the Parsonian AGIL formulation, a considerable degree of order was instituted. In addition certain other hypotheses were suggested. The process of observation and recording was by no means mechanical. The director and his assistant constantly checked their observations and discussed them with each other. The initial excitement over the Parsonian formulation gave way to a deeper understanding of its complexities and limitations as a tool for research. A concept of rewards and costs was constantly being introduced into these discussions, though the centrality of the concept did not become completely apparent for some time.

The months spent in developing a Parsonian concept of a neighborhood council were not wasted. This conception, in the form of a sixteen-fold table, proved to be an excellent classification scheme. It pointed out several aspects of the council's functioning that had been ignored. Yet, it could only alert the researchers to the problem of commitment in a council; it could not specify the relationship between commitment and the allocation of inputs or the securing of resources. Somehow the researchers had expected the sixteen-fold table to divulge the dynamics of the council. What finally became clear was that it could only be a guide. These dynamics still had to be discovered.

Epilogue

Data for the final two chapters came primarily from interviews with the Du Pont staff and key members of the various committees. Council reports and back issues of the *Du Pont News* were sources for other data. This concluding research was carried out in the late spring of 1969.

Bibliography

BOOKS

Abrahamson, Julia. *A Neighborhood Finds Itself*. New York: Harper and Bros., 1959.

Babchuck, Nicholas, and Gordon, C. Wayne. *The Voluntary Association in the Slum*. Lincoln: University of Nebraska Press, 1962.

Banfield, Edward C. *The Moral Basis of a Backward Society*. New York: Free Press, 1958.

Barnard, Chester I. *The Functions of the Executive*. Cambridge: Harvard University Press, 1938.

Blau, Peter M. *Exchange and Power in Social Life*. New York: John Wiley & Sons, 1964.

Cohen, Nathan E. *The Citizen Volunteer*. New York: Harper and Bros., 1960.

Dahl, Robert A. "The Analysis of Influence in Local Communities," *Social Science and Community Action*. Edited by Charles R. Adrian. East Lansing, Mich.: Institute for Community Development and Services, 1960.

————. *Who Governs: Democracy and Power in an American City*. New Haven: Yale University Press, 1961.

Dahrendorf, Rolf. *Class and Class Conflict in Industrial Society*. Stanford: Stanford University Press, 1959.

Dillick, Sidney. *Community Organization for Neighborhood Development*. New York: William Morrow and Company, 1953.

Etzioni, Amitai. *A Comparative Analysis of Complex Organizations*. Glencoe, Ill.: Free Press, 1961.

————, ed. *Complex Organizations*. New York: Holt, Rinehart and Winston, 1961.

Festinger, Leon; Schachter, Stanley; and Bach, Kurt. *Social Pressures in Informal Groups*. Stanford: Stanford University Press, 1950.

Foskett, John M. "The Influence of Social Participation on Community Programs and Activities," *Community Structure and Analysis*. Edited by Marvin Sussman. New York: Thomas Y. Crowell, 1959.

Gans, Herbert. *The Urban Villagers*. New York: Free Press, 1962.

Goodenough, Ward Hunt. *Cooperation in Change*. New York: Russell Sage Foundation, 1963.

Gouldner, Alvin W. "Organizational Analysis," *Sociology Today*. Edited by Robert K. Merton et al. New York: Basic Books, 1959.

————. "The Secrets of Organizations," *Social Welfare Forum, 1963*, Proceedings of the National Conference on Social Welfare. New York: Columbia University Press, 1963.

Hausknecht, Murray. *The Joiners*. New York: Bedminster Press, 1962.

Hopkins, Terence K. *The Exercise of Influence in Small Groups*. Totowa, N. J.: Bedminster Press, 1964.

Hunter, David R. *The Slums: Challenge and Response*. New York: Free Press, 1964.

Hunter, Floyd; Shaeffer, Ruth; and Sheps, Cecil G. *Community Organization: Action and Inaction*. Chapel Hill: University of North Carolina Press, 1956.

Jacobs, Jane. *The Death and Life of Great American Cities*. New York: Random House, 1961.

Johnson, Harry. *Sociology: A Systematic Introduction*. New York: Harcourt, Brace and Co., 1960.

Kahn, Alfred J. "Social Science and the Conceptual Framework for Community Organization Research," *Social Science Theory and Social Work Research*. Edited by Leonard S. Kogan. New York: National Association of Social Workers, 1960.

Kotinsky, Ruth. *Adult Education Councils*. New York: American Association for Adult Education, 1940.

Lipset, Seymour M.; Trow, Martin A.; and Coleman, James S. *Union Democracy*. Glencoe, Ill.: Free Press, 1956.

Loring, William C.; Sweetser, Frank L.; and Ernst, Charles F. *Community Organization for Citizen Participation in Urban Renewal*. Cambridge, Mass.: The Cambridge Press, 1957.

March, James G., and Simon, Herbert A. *Organizations*. New York: John Wiley & Sons, 1958.

————. "The Theory of Organizational Equilibrium," *Complex Organizations*. Edited by Amitai Etzioni. New York: Holt, Rinehart and Winston, 1961.

Merton, Robert K. *Social Theory and Social Structure*. Glencoe, Ill.: Free Press, 1957.

Meyerson, Martin, and Banfield, Edward C. *Politics, Planning and the Public Interest*. Glencoe, Ill.: Free Press, 1955.

Michels, Robert. *Political Parties*. Glencoe, Ill.: Free Press, 1949.

Parsons, Talcott. "Suggestions for a Sociological Approach to the Theory of Organizations," *Complex Organizations*. Edited by Amitai Etzioni. New York: Holt, Rinehart and Winston, 1961.

Rein, Martin, and Morris, Robert. "Goals, Structures and Strategies of Community Change," *Social Work Practice, 1962*. New York: Columbia University Press, 1962.

Reitzes, Dietrich C. "The Role of Organizational Structure: Union vs. Neighborhood in a Tension Situation," *Sociology: The Progress of a Decade.* Edited by Seymour M. Lipset and Neil J. Smelser. Englewood Cliffs, N. J.: Prentice-Hall, 1961.

Rose, Arnold. *Theory and Method in the Social Sciences.* Minneapolis: University of Minnesota Press, 1954.

Ross, Murray G. *Community Organization.* New York: Harper and Bros., 1955.

Rossi, Peter H. "Theory, Research and Practice in Community Organization," *Social Science and Community Action.* Edited by Charles R. Adrian. East Lansing, Mich.: Institute for Community Development and Services, 1960.

Sayre, Wallace, and Kaufman, Herbert. *Governing New York City.* New York: Russell Sage Foundation, 1960.

Seeley, John R. et al. *Community Chest: A Case Study in Philanthropy.* Toronto: University of Toronto Press, 1957.

Selznick, Phillip. *The Organizational Weapon: A Study of Bolshevik Strategy and Tactics.* New York: McGraw-Hill Book Company, 1952.

_____. "Foundations of the Theory of Organization," *Complex Organizations.* Edited by Amitai Etzioni. New York: Holt, Rinehart and Winston, 1961.

Sieder, Violet M. "Solving Health and Welfare Problems Through Neighborhood Participation," *The Social Welfare Forum, 1951,* Proceedings of the National Conference on Social Welfare. New York: Columbia University Press, 1951.

_____. "The Tasks of the Community Organization Worker," *Planning Social Services for Urban Needs.* New York: Columbia University Press, 1957.

_____. "What Is Community Organization Practice?" *The Social Welfare Forum, 1956,* Proceedings of the National Conference on Social Welfare. New York: Columbia University Press, 1956.

Sills, David. *The Volunteers.* Glencoe, Ill.: Free Press, 1957.

Smelser, Neil J. *Theory of Collective Behavior.* New York: Free Press, 1963.

Sower, Christopher; Holland, John; Tiedke, Kenneth; and Freeman, Walter. *Community Involvement.* Glencoe, Ill.: Free Press, 1957.

Spencer, John. *Stress and Release in an Urban Estate.* London: Tavistock Publications, 1964.

Steiner, Jesse F. "The Cincinnati Social Unit Experiment," *Community Organization in Action.* Edited by E. B. Harper and A. Dunham. New York: Association Press, 1959.

Thibaut, John W., and Kelley, Harold H. *The Social Psychology of Groups.* New York: John Wiley & Sons, 1959.

Thomas, Edwin J. "Selecting Knowledge from Behavioral Science," *Building Social Work Knowledge.* New York: National Association of Social Workers, 1964.

Truman, David B. *The Governmental Process*. New York: Alfred A. Knopf, 1960.

Vidich, Arthur J., and Bensman, Joseph. *Small Town in Mass Society*. Princeton, N. J.: Princeton University Press, 1958.

Woods, Robert A. *Neighborhood in Nation-Building*. Cambridge, Mass.: Houghton Mifflin Co., 1923.

PERIODICALS

Alexander, Chauncey, and McCann, Charles. "Concept of Representativeness in Community Organization," *Social Work*, I (January 1956), 48–52.

Arsenian, Seth, and Blumberg, Arthur. "Volunteers in the Y.M.C.A.," *Association Forum*, XL (November–December 1959), 4–9.

Becker, Howard S. "Problems of Inference and Proof in Participant-Observation," *American Sociological Review*, XXIII (December 1958), 652–60.

Berry, Margaret. "The Contribution of the Neighborhood Approach in Solving Today's Problems," *Social Service Review*, XXXVI (June 1962), 189–93.

Blackwell, Gordon W. "A Theoretical Framework of Sociological Research in Community Organization," *Social Forces*, XXXIII (October 1954), 57–64.

Carter, Genevieve W. "Practice Theory in Community Organization," *Social Work*, III (April 1958), 49–57.

Chaffee, Zacharia. "The Internal Affairs of Associations Not For Profit," *Harvard Law Review*, XLIII (May 1930), 993–1029.

Cohen, Albert K., and Hodges, Harold M. "Characteristics of the Lower-Blue-Collar Class," *Social Problems*, X (Spring 1963), 303–34.

Coleman, James. "Comment on the Concept of Influence," *Public Opinion Quarterly*, XXVII (Spring 1963), 63–82.

Coughlin, Bernard. "Community Planning: A Challenge to Social Work," *Social Work*, VI (October 1961), 37–42.

Dennis, N. "Change in Function and Leadership Renewal: A Case Study of the Community Association Movement and Problems of Voluntary Small Groups in the Urban Locality," *Sociological Research*, IX (March 1961), 55–84.

———. "Popularity of the Neighborhood Community Idea," *Sociological Review*, VI (December 1958), 191–216.

Festinger, Leon. "Behavioral Support for Opinion Change," *Public Opinion Quarterly*, XXVIII (Fall 1964), 404–17.

Form, William H. "Status Stratification in a Planned Community," *American Sociological Review*, X (October 1945), 605–13.

———. "Stratification in Low and Middle Income Housing Areas," *Journal of Social Issues*, VII, nos. 1, 2 (1951), 109–30.

Gouldner, Helen P. "Dimensions of Organizational Commitment," *Administrative Science Quarterly*, IV (March 1960), 468–90.

Holmberg, Allan R. "Participant Intervention in the Field," *Human Organization*, XIV (Spring 1955), 23–26.

Homans, George C. "Social Behavior as Exchange," *American Journal of Sociology*, LXIII (May 1958), 597–606.

Leiserson, Avery. "Problem of Representation in the Government of Private Groups," *Journal of Politics*, XI (August 1949), 66–77.

Levine, Sol, and White, Paul E. "Exchange as a Conceptual Framework for the Study of Inter-organizational Relationships," *Administrative Science Quarterly*, V (March 1961), 581–601.

Litwak, Eugene. "Voluntary Associations and Neighborhood Cohesion," *American Sociological Review*, XXVI (April 1961), 258–71.

Long, Norton E. "The Local Community as an Ecology of Games," *American Journal of Sociology*, LXIV (November 1958), 251–61.

Moe, Edward O. "Consulting with a Community System: A Case Study," *Journal of Social Issues*, XV, no. 2 (1959), 28–35.

"Neighborhood Community Organization," *Community*, XXIII (May 1948), 185–86.

Parsons, Talcott. "On the Concept of Influence," *Public Opinion Quarterly*, XXVII (Spring 1963), 37–62.

Reid, William. "Interagency Co-ordination in Delinquency Prevention and Control," *Social Service Review*, XXXVIII (December 1964), 418–28.

Rein, Martin. "Organization for Social Change," *Social Work*, IX (April 1964), 32–41.

Richardson, Hayes A. "Kansas City's People and Government Travel Together," *American City*, LXIV (February 1949), 88–90.

Schwartz, Meyer. "Our Voluntary Committee Life," *Journal of Jewish Communal Service*, XXXII (Spring 1956), 235–48.

Sills, David. "Voluntary Associations: Instruments and Objects of Change," *Human Organization*, XVIII (Spring 1959), 17–21.

Sussman, M. B. "Role of Neighborhood Association in Private Housing for Racial Minorities," *Journal of Social Issues*, XIII, no. 4 (1957), 31–37.

Thompson, James D. "Organizations and Output Transactions," *American Journal of Sociology*, LXVIII (November 1962), 309–24.

Warren, Roland L. "Toward a Typology of Extra-Community Controls Limiting Local Community Autonomy," *Social Forces*, XXXIV (May 1956), 338–41.

Webber, Melvin M. "The Politics of Information," *Trans-action*, III (November–December 1965), 41–42.

REPORTS AND PAMPHLETS

Codebook, Adult Survey. Vol. I. New York: Mobilization for Youth, 1962.

Citizen Involvement in Urban Affairs. HUD-NYU Summer Study. New York: New York University, 1968.

Dynamics of Citizen Participation. New York: National Federation of Settlements and Neighborhood Centers, 1958.

Neighborhood Acts, A: An Experiment in Cooperative Neighborhood Rehabilitation. New York: National Federation of Settlements and Neighborhood Centers, 1957.

Neighbors Unite for Better Communities. New York: United Community Funds and Councils of America, 1956.

UNPUBLISHED MATERIAL

Beck, Bertram M. "Can Agency and Client Be Coequals in Policy-Making and Administration?" Paper delivered at National Conference on Social Welfare, New York City, May 27, 1969.

Cloward, Richard A., and Piven, Frances F. "Low-Income People and Political Process." Mimeographed. New York: Mobilization for Youth, 1964.

Fox, Daniel M. "Community Corporations: Problems and Prospects." Paper delivered at National Conference on Social Welfare, New York City, May 27, 1969.

Leeds, Steven. "The Lower East Side Poverty Election." Mimeographed. New York: Columbia University School of Social Work Research Center, 1967.

Roemer, Derek V. "Focus in Programming for Delinquency Reduction." Mimeographed. Washington, D.C.: National Institute of Mental Health, 1961.

Sridharan, K. V. "Area Approach to Social Welfare Planning," Ph.D. dissertation, Ohio State University, 1959.

Index

Addams, Jane, xiv, 147
American Legion, 97
Attitudes: techniques for change of, 134n*1*

Banfield, Edward, 150
Bargaining: and staff workers, 82
Blacks. *See* Negroes
Blackwell, Gordon, 15
Blau, Peter, 19, 24
Brotherhood Week, 57, 59
Businessmen: participation of, 44

Chinese: attitude toward violence, 41n*1*; description of, 4, 7–8; political attitudes of, 8; religious attitudes of, 8; rewards sought by, 96–97
Cincinnati Social Unit Experiment, xiv
Citizen participation: costs of, 57–58, 185; effect of committee structure on, 50; effect of Poverty Program on, 158–59; exchanges and, 41n*8*; levels of, 186; norms of, 46–47, 49–50; rewards of, 171, 182; of the working class 52n*11*
City agencies, 7
Cloward, Richard, 104
Coalitions: effect on councils of, 39–40; maintenance of, 117
Coleman, James, 138, 147
Committees: membership composition of, 161; participation and structure of, 50; project selection and structure of, 101; as resources for each other, 60; staff workers and, 89
Communism, 44
Community: development of sense of, 148; factors related to sense of, 147–48; participation in, 171–72; problem solving in, 17; relevance of, 102; subsystems of, 182; surveys of needs of,

100; techniques of study of, 182
Community conflict: and community control, 174; and effect on councils, 43–44, 130; management of, 129–30
Community control: communication and, 171; community organization process and, 168; definition of, 165; degrees of, 175; of economic development, 174–75; effect on bureaucrats of, 172; idealized versions of, 173; necessity of, 176; organizational accommodations and, 143; rewards and costs of, 171–72; tactics of, 117; types of, 167
Community councils: and city departments, 70–150 passim; and community conflict, 39–40; conflicts of interest and 43–44, 68; controversy and, 17; criticism of, xviiin*4*; democratic procedures and, 149; failure of, 145; history of, xiv; ideal type of, xiii; image of, 38–39, 162; latent functions of, 118n*10*; life cycle of, 31; oligarchy in, 134n*8*; and other organizations, 109–12; participants' perceptions about, 99; programs of, 14; and project selection, 53; Protestant clergy and, 149; reform politics and, xv; research about, xvi; resources of, 164; salient rewards and, 100; structure of, 183–84; style of operation of, 138; surplus resources and, 40; survival of, 23; usefulness of, xv
—commitment to: effect on council structure of, 138; sources of, 138; symbols of, 139
—effect on: of coalitions, 39–40, 111; of elites, 123; of leadership, 44, 52n*3*; of organizations, 111–12
—functions: 146–47; as influence bank, 48–49; and organizational rivalry, 47–48; and political opportunity ladder,

211